Ploesti oil strike

John Sweetman

ßß

Editor-in-Chief: Barrie Pitt
Editor: David Mason
Art Director: Sarah Kingham
Picture Editor: Robert Hunt
Consultant Art Editor: Denis Piper
Designer: David Allen
Illustration: John Batchelor
Photographic Research: Carina Dvorak
Cartographer: Arthur Banks

Photographs for this book were especially selected from the following archives; US Air Force, US National Archives, Washington, Imperial War Museum, London, Radio Times Hulton Picture Library, London, Illustrated London News, Mansell Collection, London, Ullstein, Berlin, Suddeutscher Verlag, Munich, Staatsbibliothek, Berlin, Black Star, London, Popperfoto, London, Keystone, London, United Press London, Robert Hunt Library, London

First Printing: February 1974
Printed in United States of America

Ballantine Books Inc.

Contents

Low-level attack

Introduction by Barrie Pitt

The instruments with which Nazi Germany sought to achieve world domination could operate efficiently only so long as a supply of oil fuel was maintained. At sea, oil powered the turbines of her surface vessels and the diesels of U-boats – on land, a highly mechanised Wehrmacht spearheaded by fast-moving panzers used oil and petrol in copious quantities, while in the air, aircraft of the Luftwaffe paved the way for the ground forces in the classic Blitzkreig pattern, or razed the cities of those nations misguided enough to attempt to thwart German ambition, and to do so the aircraft had to be supplied with aviation spirit.

Much of the oil needed to run the German war machine came from Rumania. Transported by rail tanker or pumped along pipelines, crude oil from the wells flowed into the refining centre of Ploesti, situated on a tributary of the Danube and well served by roads and railways. Here it was converted into petrol, lubricants and those other derivatives essential to a modern industrial state, here also it became more vulnerable to attack.

The exploitation of Rumanian natural resources was largely financed by foreign capital and Germany had become a major investor in Rumania's industrial growth and also her largest single customer for oil between the wars. The two countries drew closer together during the years preceding 1939, although as far as the Rumanians were concerned, the situation reflected economic necessity rather than sympathy for Germany's political aims. September 1940 saw Rumania partially occupied by German troops, ostensibly to protect her oil-fields, and soon afterwards, perhaps to make more palatable the fact that she had been virtually invaded, she threw in her lot with the Axis powers.

The British had early decided that Germany's oil supplies provided a relatively easy and worthwhile target for air attack, but had mainly in mind those plants producing synthetic oil situated within Germany itself. The Ploesti refineries were also considered as targets as early as November 1940 and proposals made for bases to be set up in Greece for use by the RAF, but diplomatic considerations at that time outweighed tactical expediency, and by the time that such diplomatic niceties no longer provided a stumbling block to the enterprise, the Wehrmacht had swept through Jugoslavia and Greece and the RAF was left without airfields close enough to the target for the range of the aircraft at its disposal.

The American B24 bomber (known as the Liberator when in service with the RAF) had a long enough operating range to make an attack from bases in the Middle East a practical proposition. Unfortunately, the RAF had insufficient numbers of this type of bomber in the Mediterranean theatre to mount an effective raid on Ploesti, so the plan remained in abeyance until American-crewed B24s, diverted from China, arrived in Egypt. On 12th June 1942, thirteen of these aircraft took off from Habbaniyeh airfield in Iraq and made an attack on the refineries, causing little real damage, but showing – to both sides – that the Allies now possessed a bomber capable of making the round trip. It is safe to assume that the Germans took steps, as a result of this attack, to strengthen their defences in the area.

Although, therefore, thoughts of a decisive attack on Ploesti had been constantly in the minds of Allied planners, it was not until 1st August 1943 that a large force of B24 bombers, gathered from United States Eighth and Ninth Army Air Forces, took off from North African bases for the long flight to Rumania. By this stage in the war, the Germans had been driven westwards out of Cyrenaica by the British, and aircraft for the Ploesti attack had been concentrated on five airfields around Benghazi. The codename for the operation was changed three times. Firstly 'Statesman', it later became 'Soapsuds', and finally, perhaps in anticipation of an overwhelmingly successful attack, 'Tidalwave'.

'Tidalwave' was to be a precision raid, theoretically of the same type made by the RAF on three Ruhr dams, in May 1943, which had achieved a measure of success. But that operation had been carried out by a squadron formed and trained to drop the special mines designed by Barnes Wallis to precise requirements, while the Ploesti raid, on the other hand, was to be delivered by normal combat groups of the USAAF, one group of which had only recently flown in from the United States.

Nevertheless, by the time the raid took place, a high degree of specialised training had taken place. The crews were given an intelligence appreciation of the defences they would encounter over the target which, in the event, turned out to be inaccurate, but their comprehensive pre-attack training was extremely thorough and each crew knew its target and had practiced manoeuvres for the attack until their actions became automatic. As the proficiency of the crews increased, so also did their confidence; they were trained to a fine pitch and eager to put their newly acquired low-level techniques into practice.

That operations do not go as planned is an all-too-common occurrence in wartime. That great imponderable the weather, an unfortunate navigational error, and the fierceness of the defences combined to upset the careful planning of the raid. What was not affected by the adverse circumstances was the determination of the aircrews to press home the attack, and photographs taken during the raid show how low the pilots flew their aircraft over the target despite heavy fire from the ground; and it takes great courage to fly a cumbersome and comparatively slow bomber at only three hundred feet over a well-defended area in broad daylight. The losses suffered show that the risks taken were not insignificant.

After the raid came the post mortem – the detailed analyses of crew reports, photographs and reports from diplomatic and intelligence sources. Was the raid a success? The author has carefully sifted through all the evidence and has presented it for consideration in his final chapter – suffice it to say that he has written an intriguing account of a precision air attack from conception to final execution, and if the result did not satisfy the hopes of those who planned it – it is a story well worth the telling.

Black gold

The Libyan port of Benghasi, nestling in the Gulf of Sidra on the southern Mediterranean shore and situated some 600 miles east of Tripoli and 250 miles west of Tobruk, bore the scars of many bitter clashes during the struggle for North Africa, which had swayed back and forth between Cyrenaica and Egypt from 1940 to 1942. German, Italian, British and Commonwealth troops had all enjoyed brief periods of occupation in that process of rapid advance and retreat known locally as 'The Benghasi Handicap'.

Since November 1942, however, following General Montgomery's victory at El Alamein, Allied forces had remained there permanently; the tide of battle now flowed further west and four-engined B-24 Liberators of the United States Ninth Army Air Force had come to rest on the desert airfields south of the town. Here, on Sunday 1st August 1943, the stillness of dawn was shattered as 178 of these heavy bombers warmed up for take-off on a unique mission which involved flying a 2,700 mile round trip and attacking their target from an altitude of below 300 feet. No mission of such magnitude and difficulty had ever before been attempted.

Thick dust swirled in choking clouds over five airfields as, at two minute intervals, the aircraft took off to assemble on the line Benghasi-Tocra. Each carried 3,100 gallons of petrol and, with its supply of ammunition and bombs, weighed approximately 65,000 lbs. Several had to struggle laboriously to get airborne; for one the strain on its engines proved too much and it turned back

almost immediately. Because of the obscuring dust the pilot was unable to pinpoint the runway and land again, and the aircraft crashed killing all but two of its crew. As the remaining 177 B-24s headed over the sea towards Corfu and, far beyond, the Rumanian oil town of Ploesti, they left behind the burning funeral pyre of those who had already perished.

Crews had been thoroughly briefed on the nature of the target and known enemy defences, but as they flew northwards many reflected on the particular problems of low-level attack: balloon cables, industrial chimney stacks, the increased danger of mid-air collisions during the bombing run due to prop-wash, and even the hazard of infantry small arms fire. (Fortunately for their peace of mind they were unaware of an exercise, involving low-flying bombers and British troops manning the Benghasi harbour defences, which suggested that this latter fear was well founded.) At the final briefing, Major-General Lewis H Brereton, Commanding-General Ninth Air Force, had said: 'The American Air Forces need no spearheads in their encounters with any enemy on the face of the earth or in the sky above it . . . This is a one hundred per cent American Air Force operation'. But some crew members had also heard a more sobering exhortation from their commander: 'We expect our losses to be fifty per cent, but even though we should lose everything we've sent, but hit the target, it will be well worth it'.

Few men in that air armada had more than a superficial knowledge of Rumania, for which they were bound.

Prince Carol of Rumania

Oil is discovered in Rumania in the mid-19th century

A Royal Air Force officer, who worked with the crews during the final training period in North Africa, remarked: 'The country was unknown and might be populated by cannibals for ought they knew'. It is doubtful whether RAF personnel were any better acquainted with this distant land, part of that vague region termed in school text-books 'The Balkans' and, to British minds, akin to the comic opera kingdom of Ruritania. In 1938 the British Prime Minister had referred to a more central European state, Czechoslovakia, as 'that remote land of which we know so little', and less than a century before, when asked to become ruler of Rumania, Prince Carol reputedly sent for an atlas to see if it really existed. However, whether latterly regarded as obscure, humorous or frightening, Rumania had often occupied the stage of European politics in the past, and its importance for other nations increased still more after the discovery of crude oil there. The development of

these rich deposits explained why airmen from another continent were approaching its skies in August 1943.

Rumanian oil had first been exploited in the 19th Century before the country achieved full political independence. Long before its discovery, however, the Wallachian Plain north of the river Danube and west of the Black Sea had been an object of attention for more powerful neighbours. During the long battle for independence many international prejudices and hatreds became established, and survived to determine policies in both world wars. In some measure, therefore, Allied action against the oil industry in both conflicts was determined by longstanding historical factors.

Rumania is part of that vast trunk of land in south-eastern Europe which, hemmed in by the Adriatic, Aegean and Black Seas, hangs ponderously below Hungary. With a mixture of peoples (Greeks, Albanians, Turks, Rumanians and Slavs – the latter

9

A Bulgarian village is retaken and its inhabitants are brought before the Turkish commander, 1877

further sub-divided into Serbs, Bulgars and Croats) it has never had racial harmony and it is no accident that 'la macédoine' in French denotes a medley or mixture. Some semblance of a Rumanian state has existed since the 5th century BC, when Dacian tribesmen crossed the Danube from the south and occupied Oltenia and Banat. Threatened by Rome, Dacia was powerful enough at first to resist imperial pressure, but ultimately succumbed to the might of Trajan's armies. The forces of occupation built a stone bridge over the Danube and in the Dobruja erected a wall from the Danube to the Black Sea – remains of which survive to this day. At length the legions withdrew, and Huns and Goths arrived to pillage. Survivors of Dacia Felix, the Roman province, fled north to the hills, where some semblance of autonomy was retained.

From this rump, as the barbarian onslaught receded, developed two provinces, Moldavia and Wallachia, forming a virtual right angle resting on the north bank of the Danube, its arm (Moldavia) reaching northwards from the eastern end of the base (Wallachia). Soon, however, the Ottoman Turks in the south became aggressively hostile, defeated the provincial armies, and for three centuries Moldavia and Wallachia paid tribute to the Sultan. Although not totally absorbed into his Empire, and though later united by Prince Michael the Brave, the two provinces remained under Turkish suzerainty.

The swarthy descendants of the peoples of Dacia, renowned for their gypsy music and colourful native dress, nevertheless faced other problems. Another unfriendly neighbour, Russia, began to menace the northern borders and Austria to peer greedily over the mountains. Towards the end of the 18th Century Catherine the Great established a claim to interfere

in the provinces when Turkey (a Moslem state) recognised Russia as protector of the Christians in Moldavia and Wallachia; almost simultaneously Austria purloined Bucovina. Then, in 1812, Russia seized 17,000 square miles of Bessarabia and Moldavia, infuriating the Rumanians and creating lasting resentment.

Throughout the 19th Century the large European powers treated the Balkan peoples, nominally subject to Turkey and seeking independence from her, as a political football. Some advance towards Rumanian independence was achieved in the Treaty of Paris, but both Turkey and Austria vehemently opposed full sovereign status. In 1861, while Austria was preoccupied with her Italian territories, a state of Rumania with its capital at Bucharest was proclaimed. Sixteen years later another Russo-Turkish war gave the new state an opportunity to secure recognition of full independence and to practise that delicate mixture of bluff and diplomacy which

A Russian encampment during the Russo-Turkish war

characterised its policy for the next seventy years. Arguing that Russian success would secure Rumanian independence and that other powers would never allow the Tsar to dominate the country, Prince Carol (a Hohenzollern under whom French and German influence in Rumania increased) offered both free passage to Russian troops and military aid against Turkey. He himself led an attack on the Turkish fortress of Plevna, and the coveted independence was indeed in sight. But a price had yet to be paid. Russia demanded territory from Turkey which Rumania considered her own, and answered protests with a bald threat of war: 'The Tsar will order that Rumania be occupied and the Rumanian army disarmed.' With dignity Carol replied: 'The army which fought at Plevna may well be destroyed, but never disarmed', and Lord Salisbury, the British states-

Above: The Treaty of Peace is signed between Russia and Turkey, 1878.
Below: Bulgarian troops are mobilized during the Balkan war, 1912–13

man, expressed pro-Rumanian sympathy. Privately, however, Salisbury declared that Britain 'would not wage war for the sake of Rumania'. Russian demands were met and, at long last, in 1880 an independent kingdom of Rumania became internationally recognised. These final political machinations had only strengthened the fear and hatred of Russia, and demonstrated once more that the infant country could anticipate scant regard from larger powers unless their own interests were directly involved. Otto von Bismarck, architect of the united Germany, neatly summarised this viewpoint: 'The whole of the Balkans is not worth the bones of a single Pomeranian grenadier'.

Meanwhile south of the Danube the Bulgars were also seeking independence supported by Russia. Fearing an extension of Tsarist influence on her southern as well as northern borders and faced with Bulgarian demands for her Dobruja provinces, Rumania concluded a secret defensive alliance with Austria. Finally in 1908 Bulgaria achieved independence, but shortly afterwards became involved in two wars with other Balkan countries, during the second of which hostility between Rumania and Bulgaria hardened when the former gained southern Dobruja. In defeat the Bulgarian King declared: 'Exhausted but not vanquished we have had to furl our glorious standards in order to await better days'. Hence, on the eve of the First World War, Russia remained Rumania's hostile neighbour in the north, Bulgaria replacing Turkey in the same role to the south.

The population of Rumania in 1914 numbered about one and a half millions though, as a consequence both of loss of territory – such as Bocuvina and Bessarabia – and the preponderance of Rumanians in Hungarian Transylvania, another six millions could be counted outside the homeland. Bounded by Bulgaria, Serbia, Hungary, Russia and the Black Sea, this hilly country of forests and fertile plains stretched 350 miles east to west and 300 miles north to south. Its southern border was the river Danube, commercial artery of south-east Europe, flowing through seven countries and serving a dozen more, which makes a sharp turn northwards fifty miles short of the Black Sea and again turns east at Galatz. Thereafter, it spreads into a great delta, trapping the Dobruja province between its northward course and the Black Sea. The Wallachian Plain in the south contains good farming land where wheat and rye grow. Near the Danube rice is cultivated and further inland, when in season, the scent of tobacco flowers fills the air. The Plain gradually climbs into foothills and at length the Transylvanian Alps, which run roughly parallel to, and about 600 miles north of, the Danube. This northern mountainous region, beloved by hunters, is thickly wooded and in fact, in 1914, a quarter of Rumania was covered with a variety of conifers, beech, oak and poplar. Cutting deep into the hills are steep-sided gorges, through which streams course into pleasant grass-covered valleys and eventually drain into the Danube. Perched on the hills above are occasional fairy-tale-like castles and medieval monasteries, memories of bygone days, but useful navigational aids for Second World War airmen. On the slopes shepherds sounding, traditional long mountain horns, tend their sheep. Dobruja contains a fertile, if marshy, plain, criss-crossed with waterways and dominated by the three massive arms of the Danube Delta. Here a rich harvest of pike, carp and sturgeon can be gleaned and a multitude of colourful pelicans, swans, flamingoes and egrets observed. In the north-east of the country lies Moldavia, between the Carpathian Mountains, running along its western border, and the river Pruth. Consisting of high peaks and sheltered valleys to the west and a narrow plain to the east, it contains

the old capital of Jassy, with its ornate Orthodox churches and several attractive frescoes.

Different geographical characteristics, no less than the vagaries of history, had made the task of uniting Rumania difficult. The climate too is varied and often harsh, and frequent rain squalls make climatic conditions uncertain and liable to rapid change even in high summer, as crews on the 1943 Ploesti mission were to discover.

In the mid-19th Century, when oil (due to its commercial value soon known universally as 'black gold') was first discovered in Rumania, the overwhelming majority of the people depended upon agriculture for their livelihood: the ravages of the Industrial Revolution had not yet visited the countryside. At this time, despite the export of farming produce, reserves of national capital were small, so the industrial development which did take place in the latter half of the century relied heavily on foreign investors: in 1916 only one-sixth of the money invested in Rumanian industry originated from home sources.

The mere discovery of oil was not in itself sensational; the problem was to extract deposits in large quantities and refine them successfully, but in 1854 extraction of crude oil commenced on a commercially viable scale in Rumania. Three years later 2,000 gallons of crude oil were brought to the surface from hand-dug wells in buckets and bags. Rumanian world monopoly of oil production was short-lived, however, for in 1857 Canada dug its first successful oil well in Ontario and in the same year developed an oil refinery. Two years after a well was drilled near Titusville, Pennsylvania.

Meanwhile exploration had revealed more mineral deposits in Rumania, though only petroleum existed in large quantities. This was concentrated mainly in the foothills of the

Black gold in the foothills of the Transylvanian Alps

Transylvanian Alps, and the Prahova and Dimbovita valleys in particular became important producing areas. Petroleum (from the Latin *petra* – rock, and *oleum* – oil: the substance was originally found seeping through rocks) is now more commonly known as 'oil' and 'crude oil' as it comes from the earth. To be of value the crude oil must be refined into gasoline (petrol), lubricants, paraffin wax etc; winning the oil is only the preface to a number of complex processes. Rumanian developers soon replaced their hand-held digging implements with drills, and massive forty-foot-high wooden derricks to support them began to dot the land beside tree and cottage. As the sites increased in number and size, clusters of derricks spread in an irregular patchwork.

The business of locating refineries to serve the fields is of the utmost importance. They must be close to supplies of crude oil, within easy reach of markets or centres of distribution and near water. In Rumania Ploesti, at the mouth of the Prahova valley, beside a tributary of the Danube and the meeting point for several roadways, was an ideal choice. Here the bulk of the Rumanian oil refining industry became established.

Petroleum is made up of thousands of different combinations of hydrogen and carbon (known as hydrocarbons), which give special characteristics to its parts (or 'fractions'). Some fractions like gasoline and kerosene are valuable in themselves, but others have to be changed into useful products. So the separation and conversion of fractions constitute the main tasks of a refinery. Distillation (or fractionating) is the first step in the refining process, when separation of the various fractions takes place. Because hydrocarbons vaporise at different temperatures, it is possible to distil crude oil by passing it in a pipe through a furnace, after which the mixture of hot vapours and liquid is passed into a fractionating tower, where, as the different fractions cool, they are drawn off individually. This process, used for over half a century in Rumania, was comparatively crude and inefficient compared with thermal cracking, made available on the eve of the First World War. By this method higher octane fuel could be produced and catalytic cracking, developed in 1936, in turn produced an even higher octane petrol. The distillation and cracking plants are therefore most important and constitute prime targets for those intent upon the destruction of refinery facilities.

Rumania's comparative poverty meant that, like other branches of industry, oil had to rely upon foreign capital. Germany, for instance, did much to finance Rumanian railways and had a considerable stake in sugar, paper, cloth and cement, besides helping in the exploitation of forest land and lending support to Rumanian banks. It seemed natural, therefore, that Germany should also show an interest in oil production. In addition to foreign investments Rumania raised several state loans and by 1907 her debts to other countries totalled £57,200,000 (1,430,000,000 lei), of which £30,776,880 was owed to Germany and £18,500,000 to France. Annual payments of interest to Germany alone amounted to £2 million and by 1912 the national debt had reached £63,040,000. Furthermore, 40 per cent of Rumanian imports were financed by German banks, which required cash payment, because Germany herself took a mere 6.62 per cent of Rumanian annual exports.

Specifically, Germany had considerable interest in the oil industry. In 1903 Steaua Romana, the Rumanian state oil company, found itself in financial difficulty. As a result it came under the control of Diskonto-Gesellschaft, which put it in the hands of the Deutsche Petroleum – Atkien-Gesellschaft, whose shares were owned by leading German banks. During the next nine years further companies concerned with oil produc-

Right: German and Austro-Hungarian troops during their advance through Galizia. *Above:* Russian troops taken prisoner following the failure of the Brusilov offensive. *Below:* General Falkenhayn (left), commander of the Ninth Army on the Rumanian front

A Rumanian Maxim-gun in action

tion were founded with German money and by 1914 37 per cent of the capital invested in Rumanian oil was German, exclusive of Rumanian concerns financed by German banks. This compared with a 30 per cent overall investment in the industry by Great Britain.

At the outbreak of the First World War Rumania possessed the richest oilfields and the greatest capacity for oil production in Europe outside Russia, which, however, had greater problems of transportation to potential customers. Rumanian oil, financed mainly by Germany, Britain (Royal Dutch/Shell and Anglo-Persian Oil, then a subsidiary of Burmah Oil, now British Petroleum) and the USA (Standard Oil), officially remained under full Rumanian control and a percentage of the oil companies' profits was taken by the government.

Although comparatively young, the industry produced an annual output of over a million tons of crude oil, principally from the Campina region north of Ploesti. The larger refineries were now producing petrol, paraffin, light and heavy grade oils and vaseline, and a pipe-line ran some 150 miles from Ploesti to Constanta on the Black Sea. The annual value of the oil trade (one-half of it exported) amounted to £2 million.

But if Rumania was heavily dependent upon German financial investment to support her oil industry, then Germany also relied on Rumania to supply some of her needs in time of war. This was particularly true of oil. Attempts to produce home-manufactured benzol and low-temperature oil had failed to compensate for the lack of crude oil within Germany. Before the war 93 per cent of her mineral oil supplies came from other countries, about half from the USA and only a enth from Rumania. Once hostilities commenced, although the USA remained neutral, uncertainty about the continuation of supplies from there prompted Germany to look longingly towards the more accessible source, Rumania, which might well lack the ability to resist resolute pressure. By the accident of nature which had located oil within her borders, Rumania once more noted a powerful European nation gazing on her with rapacious intent.

In late 1914, still wary of Bulgaria and Russia, Rumania also viewed with suspicion Austro-Hungarian advances on her western neighbour Serbia and noted with trepidation the involvement of her old master, Turkey, in the international conflict. Financial ties might suggest alignment with Germany, but Rumania also had cultural and commercial links with Britain and France; and, furthermore, Hungary and Russia, with whom she disputed Transylvania and Bessarabia respectively, were ranged on different sides. Rumania therefore decided on neutrality, and to emphasise her choice forbade the export of petrol and heavy oils to belligerent counries. At first some evasion was pracised by German and Austrian companies at exorbitant cost, but after a year and with no end to the war in sight, Rumania found her stocks of refined products so high that she was compelled to allow some impartial exports to both sides. In this way refinery facilities could be made available for processing more crude oil. Germany and Austria offered goods in exchange, but Rumania insisted on cash payment; Germany was forced to pay £40 per ton for her petrol.

In the second year of the war, partly in chagrin at such treatment, Germany all but attacked Rumania. Austria had now recovered her Galician oilfields from Russia, but they provided only 50,000 tons a month, which could not satisfy the Central Powers' needs. The Ploesti

area alone refined 1½ million tons of crude oil in 1915, one-quarter of this quantity being produced as petrol. However, as long as Rumania continued to sell vital oil and grain to Germany, despite the high cost of purchase, invasion was unnecessary. Such a course would in any case be militarily unsound before Serbia had been dealt with.

Despite considerable diplomatic pressure Rumania stayed out of the war for two years. But in mid-1916, while the Russian Brusilov offensive enjoyed its momentary success, the British also briefly gained forward momentum on the Somme and the Italians (now allied to the Entente Powers) advanced in the Tyrol. Rumania then judged the time ripe for intervention and informed the French Minister in Bucharest that she would join the Allies if assistance against Bulgaria (already involved on the German side) could be assured from either Russian troops or forces from Salonika. These conditions caused considerable diplomatic heartburn and not until 17th August 1916 was a convention actually signed. By its terms Rumania promised to declare war against Austria-Hungary and launch an offensive northwards through Transylvania, Russia undertook to send three divisions into the Dobruja and Britain and France to mount an expedition from Salonika. Politically, Rumania was guaranteed the Banat, Transylvania, the Hungarian Plain up to the River Tiza and Bucovina to the River Pruth – a splendid haul which gave some indication of the worth of her oil to others. Ten days after the signing Rumania declared war on Austria-Hungary, receiving in return a rapid burst of counter-declarations from Germany, Turkey and Bulgaria.

Unfortunately for Rumania and her new allies, the Russian summer successes soon stuttered to a halt, Brusilov commenced an inglorious retreat, other Russian attacks in the north failed and the Italians were

repulsed. The Germans, too, divined Rumanian strategy. General Falkenhayn drove back their armies from the north as Field-Marshal von Mackensen crossed the Danube in the south. Although the Rumanians clung to the mountain passes south of Brasov, by 8th October they had been ejected from early conquests in Transylvania and fifteen days later Mackensen captured Constanta with its oil storage tanks full. Bucharest, the capital, fell on 6th December and soon the remnants of Rumania's tattered armies evacuated the Dobruja and withdrew to the tiny island of land in north-east Moldavia between the rivers Siret and Pruth. Rumania's brief flirtation with war was, to all intents and purposes, over. Already Germany had appointed a military Governor-General of Rumania to provide for the needs of the Central Powers 'illegally cut off' from the high seas by the British Navy. Oil figured high on his list of requisitions.

Once it became apparent that Rumanian military strength was somewhat illusory and Germany was within a hand's grasp of supplies of oil which could drastically affect the course of the whole war, the British government took steps to deny oil products to her enemies. The elementary nature of aircraft development prevented any serious consideration of bombing as a means to neutralise the wells and refineries: sabotage seemed the only choice. The Rumanians had, in fact, undertaken to destroy the installations themselves, if defeat appeared imminent and actually set up a commission to honour this undertaking. But, when the time came, the commission refused to act and Lieutenant-Colonel C B Thomson, British Military Attaché in Bucharest, informed London that,

with the Germans closing in on Ploesti, the wells and refineries remained intact.

By the third week of October, when German and Bulgarian forces entered Constanta, it was impossible to send in a body of British troops to effect destruction. Perhaps only Britain, with her penchant for the romantic hero of childhood comics, could have produced John Griffiths instead. His biography already resembled the pages of fiction. At seventeen, having served as a seaman before the mast in a windjammer, he reached Australia, where he earned a living tunnelling and mining in remote areas. He then moved to South Africa, where after a few years he established himself as an engineer, commanded a body of scouts in the Matabele War, served as a squadron leader in the South African Field Force and later on Lord Roberts' staff during the Boer War. Frequently in action, Griffiths was three times mentioned in despatches and awarded the Queen's Medal and clasp. After the war, in 1902, he resumed work as an engineering contractor. There, for most men, the story would have effectively ended, the remaining days being passed in peaceful family life.

Inactivity did not suit Griffiths, still barely thirty years old. Three years later he built the first section of the Benguela railway in Portuguese West Africa, then followed this with projects in America and directorships in British firms. In 1910 he entered the British House of Commons as Member of Parliament for Wednesbury, where, because of his preoccupation with imperial affairs, he became known as 'Empire Jack'. On the outbreak of war he organised, equipped and paid for the raising of a regiment of cavalry and shortly afterwards proposed that coal miners and other underground workers be enlisted for military mining purposes. Within a fortnight of War Office approval for this scheme he had four skeleton companies working at the front. By June 1916, as a major attached to the staff

21

The seat of the German military Governor-General in Bucharest

at General Headquarters, Griffiths had 25,000 men employed in mining activities under his control and he was largely responsible for planning the tunnelling operations under Hill 60 and the Messines Ridge. Three times mentioned in despatches, he gained the Distinguished Service Order and promotion to lieutenant-colonel. John Griffiths seemed a gift from Heaven to those faced with the urgent need to paralyse the Rumanian oil industry.

Under orders from the Director of Military Intelligence and armed with an undertaking from the Treasury that Britain would compensate for damage to machinery and installations, Griffiths set out for Bucharest. Incredibly, he travelled by British warship to Norway, thence by land and sea to Moscow via Sweden and Finland. From Moscow he and his batman (his sole travelling companion) went by train to the Rumanian frontier. Finding no official trans-

port there he commandeered a car at gunpoint and drove to the capital, arriving on 13th November 1916 having completed an exhausting 4,000 miles in nineteen days. German troops were less than one hundred miles away and panic-stricken refugees thronged the cobbled streets of Bucharest. Griffiths found the government unimpressed by guarantees of compensation, and that commercial interests, Royal Dutch/Shell and Standard Oil for instance, were prepared to obstruct him.

Seeing no future in negotiations at Bucharest, with the Germans converging from most points of the compass, Griffiths travelled some thirty-five miles north to Ploesti, then north-west to Targoviste situated at the foot of the mountains. Here he met the Rumanian Oil Commission, which bluntly refused to destroy oil installations, even if the Allies suffered thereby. Privately, however, Griffiths was assured of support from the royal family.

He now laid plans for the systematic destruction of the Rumanian oil in-

John Norton-Griffith, saboteur of the Rumanian oilfields in 1916

dustry, based on advice from London suggesting the use of British personnel working in the oilfields. At a British-controlled plant near Targoviste he signed a guarantee of compensation on behalf of the British government and secured the necessary men to assist him in his task. Families were evacuated, deep channels were dug to the refinery and flooded with petrol, which was then fired. Parties were sent out to other oilfields and refineries to hack down derricks, throw metal blocks and rubbish down wells and blow up pipelines, as Griffiths moved south once more. The Steaua Romana refinery at Campina and Astra Romana at Ploesti were flooded with petrol and ignited: both were to be prime targets on 1st August 1943. Griffiths just managed to keep ahead of the German cavalry in his requisitioned car, though on one occasion he found himself arrested by the Rumanian Oil Commission, as anxious to stop him ravaging their valleys as were the Germans. Once more production of his pistol proved effective and he escaped.

Thus, on the day that Mackensen entered Bucharest, clouds of belching black smoke darkened the northern sky. Two hundred square miles of land were alight and as Griffiths moved off he knew that immediate oil supplies had been denied to the Germans. One man had destroyed Rumanian production capacity and wrought £56 million of damage. By mid-1918, eighteen months later, the Germans claimed to have restored two-thirds production, but a more realistic figure would be 15 per cent. General Falkenhayn estimated that these lost supplies were equivalent to a major military defeat in the field.

For his exploits Griffiths (in 1918 he assumed the name Norton-Griffiths) was created a Knight Companion of the Bath and officer of the Legion of Honour, and received too the Star of Rumania and the Order of St Vladimir of Russia (Third Class). In an attempt to repeat his achievements in the Second World War the Allies needed to despatch nearly 2,000 airmen.

Frustrated plans

Although King Ferdinand retained political control over the tiny remnants of his kingdom once his defeated army retreated across the River Siret, he did so by courtesy of Russia, for which Rumanians felt such long-standing hatred. When Tsar Nicholas II abdicated in March 1917, however, Ferdinand encouraged a lessening of hostility among his people towards their protectors, in the hope that the new Russian government would actively help to recover lost Rumanian territory. He also promised land reform in Rumania to fire national enthusiasm for the task of reconquest.

But neither the Russian nor Rumanian armies proved anxious to renew battle, and in October Lenin and the Bolsheviks, pledged to achieve peace, seized control in Petrograd. Shortly afterwards Russia signed an armistice with the Central Powers, to which Rumania inevitably adhered.

Any slender hope that renewal of hostilities might occur and enable Ferdinand to regain his whole kingdom was soon dashed. In March 1918 Lenin concluded the Treaty of Brest

King Ferdinand and Queen Maria attend a banquet in Bucharest

...itovsk, which took Russia out of the war. Left defenceless Rumania was then obliged to sign the humiliating Treaty of Bucharest, which disarmed much of her army and gave the bulk of its equipment to the Central Powers. Nominally the Rumanian royal family would rule Moldavia from Jassy. This left the oil industry of Wallachia in enemy hands.

Ironically, therefore, Griffiths' work proved beneficial to the Germans, who could replace damaged machinery with their own. More effective overall control of the oil industry by them also came about. Rumania was required to sign a Petroleum Agreement supplementary to the political provisions of the Treaty of Bucharest. As a result virtually all railways, rich farmlands and oil installations (both in fields and refineries) came under Germany and Austria-Hungary. A new Oil Fields Leasing Company obtained extensive and exclusive rights for thirty years, with an option of renewal for two further periods of the same length. A maximum of one-quarter of the company's shares would be offered to the Rumanian government, which might transfer them to private companies if it so desired. However, Germany and Austria-Hungary assured themselves of a controlling influence by creating preference shares with a fifty-fold voting value, which were to remain exclusively at their disposal. A series of complicated provisions gave the Oil Fields Leasing Company possession of all equipment, the power to fix prices and practically absolute freedom from taxes: the Rumanian government received merely four lei (about 15p) per ton for exported oil products and 3.40 lei for exported crude oil.

The events of 1916-18, therefore, had a considerable effect upon the Rumanian oil industry, whose development would have taken a far different course if the Central Powers had not at length been defeated in western Europe. Not until their collapse did the Rumanian government sally forth from the confines of Jassy. On 1st December 1918 the King finally re-entered the capital from which he had fled two years earlier to find that restoration and rehabilitation would be assisted by one significant fact. Despite her lack of military distinction and fleeting appearance in the lists, Rumania had backed the winning side. So from the peace settlements she emerged greatly enlarged. Through acquisition of Transylvania, Bucovina and Bessarabia, Rumania doubled her territory and population. Nonetheless, even with possession of industrial concerns in Transylvania and Bucovina a mere 10 per cent of the population in 'Greater Rumania,' as it became known, was employed in industry; and pressure for land reform remained an important factor in Rumanian affairs, for 75 per cent of rural holdings in the country were still less than five hectares (12½ acres) and many consisted of scattered strips served by poor agricultural methods. With Hungary, Russia and Bulgaria openly hostile and committed to recovering their lost provinces, Rumania relied heavily upon Allied political support after the First World War; moreover, like most war-torn European countries, she needed to borrow extensively from others.

The post-war settlements left Rumania with one very serious domestic problem. She inherited a number of racial minority groups with her new territories: Transylvania had over two million Magyars and Germans, Bessarabia a half a million Ukranians and the Dobruja a quarter of a million Bulgarians. So one-quarter of her population was non-Rumanian in origin. In common with other states which acquired similar minorities, Rumania guaranteed 'full and complete protection of life, race and liberty to all inhabitants without distinction of birth, nationality, language, race or religion'. But, concentration on commercial ventures in

The arrival of the Russian delegation, (Trotsky centre profile) at Brest Litovsk

old Rumania and development of a communications system designed to serve Bucharest rather than outlying regions, failed to persuade minorities in Rumania that this pledge would be honoured. In 1921 Rumania, Czechoslovakia and Jugoslavia signed the so-called Little Entente for mutual defence against nations who might try to use minority dissatisfaction for revision of the peace settlements, and an alliance was also concluded with France.

There were other worries at home too. Peasant small-holders suffered in the years of post-war economic depression and mounting industrial unrest caused particular concern. The Rumanian Communist Party was officially founded during these difficulties at Ploesti in 1922. Although at first exercising little political influence, it did profit from the government's ruthless repression of strikes and demonstrations, especially after several workers had been killed in an incident at Lupin in 1929. Nor did the activities of the royal family assist political stability at this time. The dissolute heir to the throne, Carol, renounced all claims to his inheritance and left the country to indulge in pleasures elsewhere. Then three years after the accession of his young son (later to visit American prisoners of war after the Ploesti raid) the exile organised a coup in Rumania, deposed Michael and returned to rule himself in 1930.

Within five years of Carol's accession Hitler's behaviour in Germany and his cavalier treatment of the League of Nations were causing serious misgivings in the Balkan peninsula, although the mutual hatreds and jealousies among its nations precluded any significant self-protective measures. An agreement between

News vendors race to spread word of the armistice in Bucharest

Turkey, Jugoslavia, Greece and Rumania in 1934 was so hedged with provisions and seriously weakened by the non-adherence of Bulgaria that the possibility of German political and military intervention in the Balkans again seemed real. Consequently Rumania re-established diplomatic relations with Russia (now the USSR). In the meantime a pro-fascist organisation, the Iron Guard, which undertook to ally with Germany and Italy once in power, was gaining influence within Rumania and rivalled the Communists. But through a series of adroit manoeuvres Carol II had achieved virtual dictatorial power by 1938, when he set off on a European tour. Convinced that Britain and France would ultimately triumph if war occurred, he was nevertheless determined to strengthen links with Hitler by way of insurance cover. So it was reported of Carol's meeting with Hitler: 'The King of Rumania ... desired especially to maintain and consolidate the good relations with

Above: **King Carol and Prince Michael.** *Below:* **A fascist meeting in 1934, when the fascists were beginning to gain influence in Rumania.** *Right:* **Funeral of Iron Guard leaders who were shot 'whilst trying to escape'**

the German Reich that existed today'.

This blissful co-existence was short-lived. Soon after Carol returned home, the imprisoned Iron Guard leaders were shot, ostensibly whilst trying to escape. The Führer's anger was mollified only by Rumanian willingness to grant Germany economic concessions, one of which involved expansion of the Junker aircraft factory at Brasov. This was not an isolated example of economic interest, for by the outbreak of the Second World War Germany had a considerable financial stake in Rumania through a variety of enterprises from soya beans to silver mines. Wheat exports from Rumania to Germany increased enormously in the 1930s and Germany sought to make Rumania reliant upon her for some manufactured goods by refusing their production under licence. In March 1939 a bilateral trade treaty allowed for the establishment of new joint companies to exploit natural resources in Rumania, to which France reacted by signing a trade

The developing Rumanian oil industry, subject of close attention from Germany

treaty with Rumania, and Britain by hastily despatching a trade mission to Bucharest. Yet, despite all the efforts of France and Britain, by 1939 39.3 per cent of Rumania's imports came from Germany, which in turn received 32.3 per cent of her exports. A special cause for concern was Rumanian reliance on Germany for supplies of arms. In fact Rumania had very little choice in the matter, for Germany decreed that payment for certain goods and materials received from other countries should be in arms not cash.

The oil industry attracted particular attention from Germany. In 1935 Germany took 600,000 tons from Rumania and thus became her biggest single customer. Reacting swiftly, France agreed to purchase 750,000 tons annually and so surpass Germany as top customer. This game of economic leap-frog was conducted against the background of perennial foreign control of Rumanian oil: for of the £14.5 million share capital of the 150 companies involved, a mere 9.7 per cent represented home investment. Moreover, although at the start of the war Germany was receiving only one-third of her oil imports from Rumania, it was significant that Rumania's total oil exports exceeded German needs in time of peace. But it was unlikely that Rumania alone could satisfy Germany's requirements in war: her annual output had risen from some five million tons in 1929 to just short of eight million in 1936, but the total tonnage for 1938 was only 6½ million: this suggested that production might well have passed its peak. In 1937 Germany imported just over 3½ million tons of oil products.

A pro-German Cabinet takes office and Iron Guard members openly parade the streets of the capital, 1940

At the opening of the Second World War, as in 1914 therefore, Rumania was commercially and financially committed to Germany to a considerable degree, but sentimentally attached to Britain and France. This was particularly true of the latter, whose commune system provided the model for Rumanian local government and whose influence could be seen in Bucharest's own Arc de Triomphe and the social habits of the Rumanian upper classes. The defeat of France and the anticipated fall of Britain in mid-1940 denuded Rumania of strong support in the international arena, although official relations were maintained with both Britain and Vichy France. The USSR soon took the opportunity of demanding the secession of Bessarabia and Bucovina: not surprisingly, considering Hitler's current friendship with Stalin, an appeal for help to Berlin by Rumania failed. The two provinces were surrendered without a fight, Rumania renounced the Anglo-French guarantee of 1938, a pro-German Cabinet took office and Iron Guard members openly strutted the streets. Hard upon the Russian demands came those of Bulgaria and Hungary who, after Germano-Italian 'mediation' at Vienna, received southern Dobruja and 17,000 square miles of Transylvania respectively. In two months Rumania had forefeited one-third of her territory, three million Rumanian and two million non-Rumanian subjects. It was cold comfort to hear Germany and Italy guarantee that which remained. Although Carol II was forced to abdicate in favour of his son Michael, Rumania's dangerous political weakness did not improve, for real power lay with the pro-fascist Prime Minister General Ion Antonescu. The few remaining British engineers were now ejected from the oilfields, sometimes after physical ill-treatment. Interestingly, however, Hitler refused an

General Antonescu, right, and King Michael

Italian request for full-scale intervention in the Balkans, for fear that Britain might establish bases on the peninsula from which she could bomb the oil installations.

In September 1940 German troops entered Rumania, officially as a military mission after a request from Antonescu for assistance to protect vital industrial plants. Already Hitler had become alarmed at the deterioration of German relations with the USSR and was acutely aware that, after the occupation of Bessarabia, Russian airfields were a mere hundred miles from Ploesti. Significantly, when granting transit rights through her territory to German troops, Hungary noted that their aim was to protect the Rumanian oilfields. In spite of efforts to disguise the fact, effectively Rumania had been occupied; and shortly afterwards together with Hungary she adhered to the Tripartite Pact of co-operation between Germany, Italy and Japan.

The Rumanian oil industry was soon brought under close German control. The Kontinentale Company, a German concern whose shares were owned by German industrialists and the German government, was set up to administer expropriated foreign companies and Germany rapidly took over responsibility for Rumanian railways and traffic on the Danube. Rioting in Bucharest in January 1941, suppressed by German tanks, enabled an overt extension of the Axis presence; and, as some 500,000 German troops were now in the country, the British diplomatic position became untenable. On 14th February 1941 relations between Britain and Rumania were severed, creating widespread, but erroneous, fear that air attack on the oilfields was imminent. Not until 7th December did Britain actually declare war, and three days later Rumania did so on the USA. Meanwhile in June 1941 Rumania had joined Germany in a 'holy war' against her old Russian antagonist and during the opening phases of

German troops officially enter Rumania following a request from Antonescu for assistance to protect industrial plants

Operation Barbarossa had recovered Bucovina and Bessarabia. It was the rejection of a virtual ultimatum by Britain to withdraw west of the Dniester following further advances, which led to the declaration of war and spurred Britain to think once more of a way to stop Rumanian oil from reaching Germany.

Inevitably, in connection with this objective, Ploesti attracted special attention. Standing 160 miles west of the Black Sea and seventy miles north of the Danube, the town lies at the mouth of the Prahova valley some thirty-five miles north-west of Bucharest and fifty miles south-east of Brasov, where the Wallachian Plain begins to climb towards the Transylvanian Alps. Archaeological remains suggest some sort of human habitation in the Bronze Age, but not until 1503 does Ploesti appear on maps as a village, traditionally deriving its name from a father and his seven sons who fled there from Transylvania. Almost another hundred years passed before it achieved town status under Michael the Brave. Located at co-ordinates 44° 56′N, 26° 02′E, Ploesti is officially shown as 165 metres above sea level, but its height actually varies from 184 to 158 metres north to south and from 197 to 157 metres west to east – important variations when considering a minimum-altitude air attack. The population in 1941 was 100,000, though the Germans soon evacuated all non-essential personnel. Its industrial districts covered some nineteen square miles. In the early years of the Second World War the town consisted of neat rows of streets and wide boulevards (such as Independence Boulevard leading straight from the centre to Ploesti South

The town centre of Ploesti

station), lined with trees and white, single-storeyed houses, with the residential sky-line punctuated by church spires, factory chimneys and oil derricks. From the central square, where two prominent Orthodox churches and a statue commemorating the foundation of Rumania stood, twelve main roads led outwards to towns like Pitesti, Buzau, Bucharest and Constanta. Viewed from the air, the lay-out of Ploesti roughly resembled a wheel of four miles diameter with the roads as spokes and railway lines, which encircled the entire town, representing the outer rim.

The town was dominated by oil refineries, which in turn ringed it outside the surrounding railways. Beyond the refineries lay fields, where corn and root crops were cultivated. Some two miles north-east of the town flowed the half-mile wide river Teleajen, a tributary of the Ialomita which drains into the Danube on its northward course to Galatz. Running north-west to south-east through

Ploesti ; dominated by oil refineries and surrounded by fields

Ploesti itself ran the smaller River Dambul. In addition to the several roads, six railway lines led off from the circle of tracks, which connected the refineries on the edge of the town with oilfields and other towns in Rumania.

Eighteen miles north-west of Ploesti on the railway line to Brasov lay Campina, where the Steaua Romana refinery stood. Three miles south of Ploesti on the west of the line to Bucharest and shaped like an irregular arrowhead ¾ mile by ½ mile lay the Credituel Minier refinery in the suburb of Brazi. On the northern edge of Ploesti itself was the 240-acre Concordia Vega refinery, immediately east of the railway to Valenii de Munte. A half mile south-east of this, also outside the surrounding railway track, stood two small refineries, Cometa and Redeventa, within a

40-acre complex; and a further three-quarters of a mile south-east from them was the minor Dacia Romana plant. West of the town, half way between the railways to Campina and Valenii de Munte, was the isolated Xenia refinery of some eighty acres, close to Ploesti North-West station. On the south side of the town stood a cluster of refineries: Columbia Aquila, 160 acres, inside the circle of tracks – the only refinery so placed – close to Ploesti West station, separated by a half mile and the railway to Brazi and Bucharest from a vast irregularly-shaped complex to the east, which contained the Astra Romana, Unirea Orion and Lumina refineries. In turn a half mile further east lay another complex spread over 160 acres, containing the Standard Petrol Block and Unirea Sperentza: between these latter two complexes lay Ploesti South station, its extensive marshalling yards themselves an inviting target. Situated between the refineries around Ploesti were several boosting and pumping stations. One refinery stood utterly alone. Romana Americana, covering 400 acres, was three quarters of a mile north-east of Teleajen station, itself three miles from the centre of Ploesti and one mile beyond the surrounding railway tracks.

In order of importance seven of these refineries could be considered worthwhile targets. Astra Romana, originally controlled by Royal Dutch/ Shell, had a modern cracking unit capable of producing 87 octane aviation fuel. Within its confines was an important pumping station for the Giurgiu pipe-line; and close by were the junction of railway lines to Campina, Bucharest and Buzau and the Ploesti South station with its large marshalling yards. Then came Concordia Vega, formerly controlled by French and Belgian interests, and the only Rumanian refinery with cracking equipment capable of producing high grade lubrication oil; furthermore, most vitally, within its confines were pumping installations which distributed all crude oil coming from the oilfields to the other refineries in Ploesti. Romana Americana, once US-controlled, contained extremely modern equipment, cracking units and the power plant for the pumping station which served the Constanta pump-line; and the ex-British Unirea Orion, although comparatively small, had modern cracking installations and was responsible for the bulk (though not the best) of the lubricating oil produced in the area. Next in importance came Unirea Sperantza, also ex-British, adjoining the Standard Petrol Block, formerly American, both of which contained cracking and lubricating oil plants. Finally in Ploesti itself, Columbia Aquila, built by an American and British consortium but French controlled, produced a high proportion of the total benzine output of Rumania and, with its cracking units and important boiler house, made a compact target.

At Campina Steaua Romana was one of the largest and most modern refineries in Rumania, previously financed by the Anglo-Iranian Oil Company, with an efficient cracking unit and the only important paraffin-wax plant in the country. Then, in the southern suburb of Brazi Credituel Minier was located. Possessing up-to-date cracking units, it was the one refinery capable of producing 100 octane aviation fuel. Because all these refineries had previously been owned, managed or served by Allied experts, accurate information about their lay-out and the position of vital cracking, boiler and distillation units could be readily obtained.

Surprisingly, in view of Rumania's pre-war trade with Europe, in 1938 85 per cent of Rumanian oil exports went through Constanta, 10 per cent via the Danube and 5 per cent along the three main railways into central Europe. In time of war, however, exit into the Mediterranean through the Dardanelles was liable to be blocked by naval action, consequently the importance of Constanta declined and Giurgiu (on the Danube eighty miles south-west of Ploesti) became the main centre for distribution to Europe. A minimum of four pipe-lines took oil from Ploesti to Giurgiu, but this route carried only one-quarter of the amount sent by rail: for all major Ploesti refineries had their own railway sidings and a double-tracked line ran from the town to Giurgiu. Thus the railway bridges and Danube barges could also constitute important secondary targets.

Whatever the difficulties there were powerful arguments for interrupting supplies from the Ploesti refineries to Germany. Before the outbreak of war considerable attention had been given to Germany's sources of oil supply. In August 1938 an official British estimate put her oil imports from all sources at 4¼ million tons, which might well need to be doubled in time of war. Her total supplies were just over seven million tons, though only

552,000 tons of crude oil, mainly from Westphalia, and 1,600,000 of synthetic products originated within Germany's own borders. Hopefully, once war was declared, a naval blockade would deny to Germany all external supplies, with the exception of those from Rumania and the USSR (about 180,000 tons per month in all). In fact, Rumania constituted a much greater prize than the 1938 figures suggest, for total output was 9.7 million tons. Capture of the Rumanian oil industry would therefore go far towards satisfying Germany's estimated war requirements of 11,700,000 tons per year – although this forecast was partly invalidated by acquisition of 1½ million tons of oil during the European campaigns of 1940 and discovery of the Prinzendorf oilfield in the Vienna Basin, which helped to boost production from the Austrian provinces to over a million tons by the end of 1942.

Oil is transported from the refineries by rail

Until the outbreak of war eighty-five per cent of Rumanian oil was exported from Constanta

Within days of the commencement of war in September 1939, the British government decided on immediate purchase of surplus oil stocks in Rumania to pre-empt Germany, on the assumption that 'the restriction of Germany's supplies . . . may shorten the war, not by weeks, but by months'. This plan ran into difficulty, however, with the Rumanians' demanding payment in dollars and the British at first unwilling to comply; and it soon became apparent that German influence at Bucharest was even greater than hitherto suspected. Ultimately payment in unconvertible sterling was agreed and British companies were authorised to offer 50 per cent above Gulf prices. Towards the end of 1939 a certain amount of buying did take place and several long-term contracts were signed. Unfortunately for

Mr Geoffrey Lloyd

Britain, just when this programme appeared likely to succeed, Rumania suddenly rationed oil exports. It now became clear that she had reached a firm agreement with Germany on the supply of oil and, despite direct Anglo-French interest in the oil industry, Rumania was yielding to German pressure concerning exports to other countries.

Pre-emption thus having failed, Britain tried diplomatic action. Rumania was asked for full details of all her commercial transactions with Germany and, in the light of the reply, Britain would review the extent of her own trade with Rumania. Meanwhile, because Germany relied heavily upon the Danube barges to carry most of her oil supplies from Rumania, plans were laid to purchase or charter as many of them as possible. For this purpose the Goeland Company was established. By the end of 1939, out of 382 tugs, 2,039 barges and 304 tankers of all countries using the river, 148 vessels had been char-

Sir Charles Portal

Sir Richard Peirse

tered. This comparative lack of success through peaceful means to stop oil traffic on the Danube prompted consideration of more extreme measures, such as use of explosives to block the river or despatch of an expeditionary force to Rumania, all of which were rejected as militarily unsound. The Rumanian government, undoubtedly prodded by Germany, soon adopted a hostile attitude both towards the Goeland Company and Allied commercial concerns within Rumania. Britain reacted in turn by seizing certain Rumanian assets in the United Kingdom and withholding goods destined for Rumania. It was by now apparent that commercial and diplomatic attempts to deny oil to Germany must end in failure, and thoughts inevitably turned to a more physically active course.

Even before the German attack on western Europe in May 1940, the French Prime Minister had suggested bombing Russian oilfields in the Caucasus to prevent supplies going to Germany; and shortly after the panzers advanced into the Low Countries, the British Ministry of Economic Warfare agreed that an air offensive on the Rumanian oilfields would be desirable. The RAF did bomb synthetic oil plants in Germany which, through the Bergius hydrogenation and Fischer-Troppau processes and the use of coal, produced 90 per cent of all the high octane aviation fuel used by Germany. An air assault on these plants, many of which were within reach of British bombers operating from their home bases even after the fall of France, promised a lucrative return for effort. In June 1940 the British Air Staff thought that a reduction of her oil reserves by 500,000 tons during the next three months would make the position 'extremely critical' for Germany and a month later emphasised that 'oil targets are very vulnerable'. Consequently in July it was officially laid down that '. . . oil is the weakest link in Germany's war economy . . . (and)

the destruction of Germany's oil resources remains the basis of the main offensive strategy towards the reduction and dislocation of Germany's war potential,' with the added hope that oil targets could be 'seriously damaged by a relatively light scale of attack'.

Encouragement for the view that RAF bombing against synthetic oil plants could be both accurate and decisive was forthcoming when a committee under Mr Geoffrey Lloyd concluded in December 1940 that a mere 539 tons of bombs (6.7 per cent of RAF Bomber Command's total effort) had reduced German synthetic oil output by 15 per cent. This prompted Sir Charles Portal, Chief of the Air Staff, to conclude that destruction of the seventeen major synthetic oil plants within six months would deny Germany 1½ million tons of oil. This loss would render action against Rumania unnecessary, though Lloyd wrote: 'The only way to get a quick death clinch on the whole enemy oil position is to destroy the synthetic plants and to intercept Rumanian supplies'. A little later Lloyd suggested initiating sabotage in Rumania, because the oil industry was beyond the range of existing British bombers. Early in the new year RAF Bomber Command was informed 'that the sole primary aim of your bomber offensive, until further notice, should be the destruction of the German synthetic plants,' and Sir Richard Peirse, Air Officer Commanding RAF Bomber Command, expressed confidence that 'we shall be able to do what is necessary'. Unfortunately, for a number of reasons, his confidence proved misplaced. It quickly became evident that Lloyd's calculations of damage were grossly exaggerated. Reconnaissance on Christmas Eve 1940 after two plants at Gelsenkirchen had been attacked by 296 aircraft dropping 262 tons of bombs (exclusive of incendiaries) revealed no obvious damage, and during one night in February 1941 only six out of twenty-two Hampdens and seven out of forty-four Wellingtons even claimed to have attacked their designated oil targets. Navigational problems, the strength of enemy defences and mechanical failures partly accounted for these disappointing results, and the British decision to concentrate on night raids to reduce aircraft losses did not assist bombing accuracy. In April 1941 the British Air Staff accepted an average bombing error of 1,000 yards at night and 300 yards by day, and four months later an official report concluded that only one-third of all RAF bombers believed to have reached their targets (not exclusively the oil plants) had actually got within five miles of them and that over the Ruhr the total was one-tenth. Weather conditions, moreover, drastically curtailed the number of bombing missions. Sir Charles

Prime Minister Winston Churchill inspects shore defences

Portal had calculated the need for 3,400 sorties to cripple the seventeen major synthetic plants within four months: yet in six months, spanning the last quarter of 1940 and the first in 1941, only 646 were flown.

It therefore appeared depressingly obvious that, for the present, decisive results against German synthetic oil plants could not be attained. In April 1942 Colonel Oliver Stanley, British Secretary of State for the Colonies, concluded that current capability precluded a satisfactory end to this programme. He thus reinforced a recent Ministry of Economic Warfare appraisal that reduction of the Axis oil output by less than 100,000 tons per month would have no real value. Early in 1942 a new navigational aid for aircraft, Gee, had become available and hope of successful action was rekindled. Sir Charles Portal rapidly killed such aspirations. He estimated that, even if all ten plants within Gee range were destroyed, only 7.6 per

cent of German production would be affected, and with operational difficulties this might more realistically be considered a mere 1 per cent.

Once it was evident that the synthetic plants could not be neutralised, direct action against the Ploesti area became a matter for more serious discussion. Before the end of 1940 the British had considered the possibility of air action. On 27th November Winston Churchill, the Prime Minister, addressed a personal minute to the Chief of the Air Staff, admitting that the future military and political situation in south-east Europe was uncertain, but suggesting that 'we should at once begin to establish in Greece ground staff and nucleus stores (sic) to enable at least two squadrons of Wellingtons to bomb the Rumanian oilfields,' adding: 'We are late enough already in making these preparations. They certainly should not be put off any longer'. Next day Sir Charles Portal contacted RAF authorities in Cairo and Greece, pointing out that if Bulgarian neutrality should be violated, Rumanian oilfields might have to be bombed at short notice: he instructed that necessary arrangements be made for two squadrons of Wellingtons to execute this task, suggesting the use of airfields on the Greek islands of Lemnos and Mitylene in the Aegean Sea. The same day in London, Portal agreed that the oilfields constituted poor targets, but refineries around Ploesti would be 'very good targets'. Accordingly, he drew the attention of the Director of Plans to the fact that maps of the area had been made available 'some time ago' and instructed that a feasibility study be worked out in conjunction with oil experts to decide the size of bombs, fuse settings etc, necessary to complete a successful bombing mission.

Early in January 1941 Anthony Eden, British Secretary of State for Foreign Affairs, submitted an appreciation on the subject. He noted that bombing or sabotage were possible means of dealing with the Rumanian oil industry. If bombing were chosen withdrawal of the British Minister from Bucharest would be necessary, and any attack from Greece would violate either Jugoslavian or Bulgarian air space to the embarrassment of diplomatic representatives there. On the other hand, a bombing attack needed surprise for success and withdrawal of a minister from any of these countries might alert defences to impending hostile action. Eden continued that 'if bombing is not immediately practicable, sabotage, the complementary means, must become the alternative and be exploited to the full,' and implied that this method would avoid unpleasant international reaction to a pre-emptive air strike. 'The time factor and surprise are all important and must not be prejudiced by diplomatic action unrelated to the stern realities of war,' he continued. He hoped that, if caught, saboteurs would not reveal their masters, hence if sabotage were used the British Minister would not need to leave Rumania. Alas, John Griffiths was not on hand to advise upon the technicalities of any such attempt. His death had been as bizarre as his life. In 1930 he committed suicide in a surf boat off Alexandria, in the same year that the former Military Attaché, who had supported him in Bucharest, perished in the R101 airship disaster.

By 28th January 1941 a detailed appreciation of the RAF's capacity to attack Ploesti was ready. Three Wellington and two Blenheim squadrons were available and could be accommodated at Larisa and Athens (Menidi and Eleusis), with Salonika (Sedes) suitable for advanced refuelling if required. Ploesti, Bucharest and Giurgiu were within range of these airfields, but for night operations over the mountains good weather, anticipated on only ten to twelve nights in both February and March, was needed. Using 500-lb bombs an approximate monthly load would be 258 tons, but, bearing in mind navigational and

bombing problems already experienced in Europe which would reduce the tonnage actually dropped on a target, four months would be necessary to achieve the planned objective. This rather gloomy prediction was not assisted by information from the British Minister in Bucharest that Rumania possessed two to three times more refinery capacity than she actually had in use.

Appended to this operational appreciation was a list of targets in order of importance, based upon the amount of crude oil each processed during 1939. First came the Astra Romana complex at Ploesti (1,844,000 tons), with the additional attraction that the town's main marshalling yards were close by, then Concordia Vega (996,000), Romana Americana (797,000), Steaua Romana at Campina (600,000), the Danube loading wharf at

Blenheims, also made available for the planned attack

Giurgiu, which was considered highly inflammable, and the Prahova refinery at Bucharest (186,000), also alongside important marshalling yards. Lord Hankey, Chancellor of the Duchy of Lancaster and chairman of an official British committee concerned with German oil supplies, raised the possibility of attacking Ploesti with Sir Charles Portal early in February, qualifying his own proposition by noting that the Rumanian oil targets were too scattered for effective action by the small RAF forces in Greece and that the neutrality of Balkan nations created an important stumbling block. A Foreign Office paper of 12th February announced the imminent withdrawal of the British Minister from Bucharest (effected two days later) and noted that the Cabinet was seriously considering an air attack on the Rumanian oil resources. The Foreign Office thought such consider-

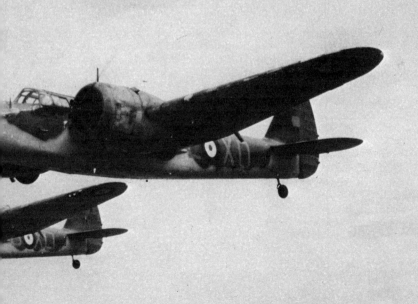

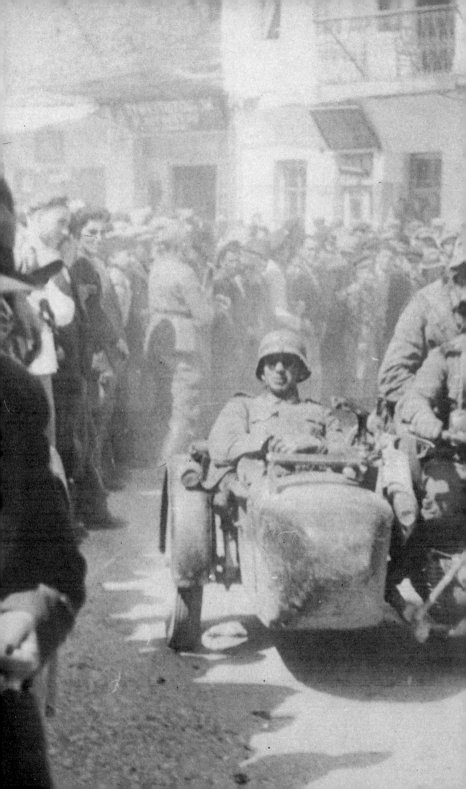

German motorcycle troops enter
Greece, April 1941

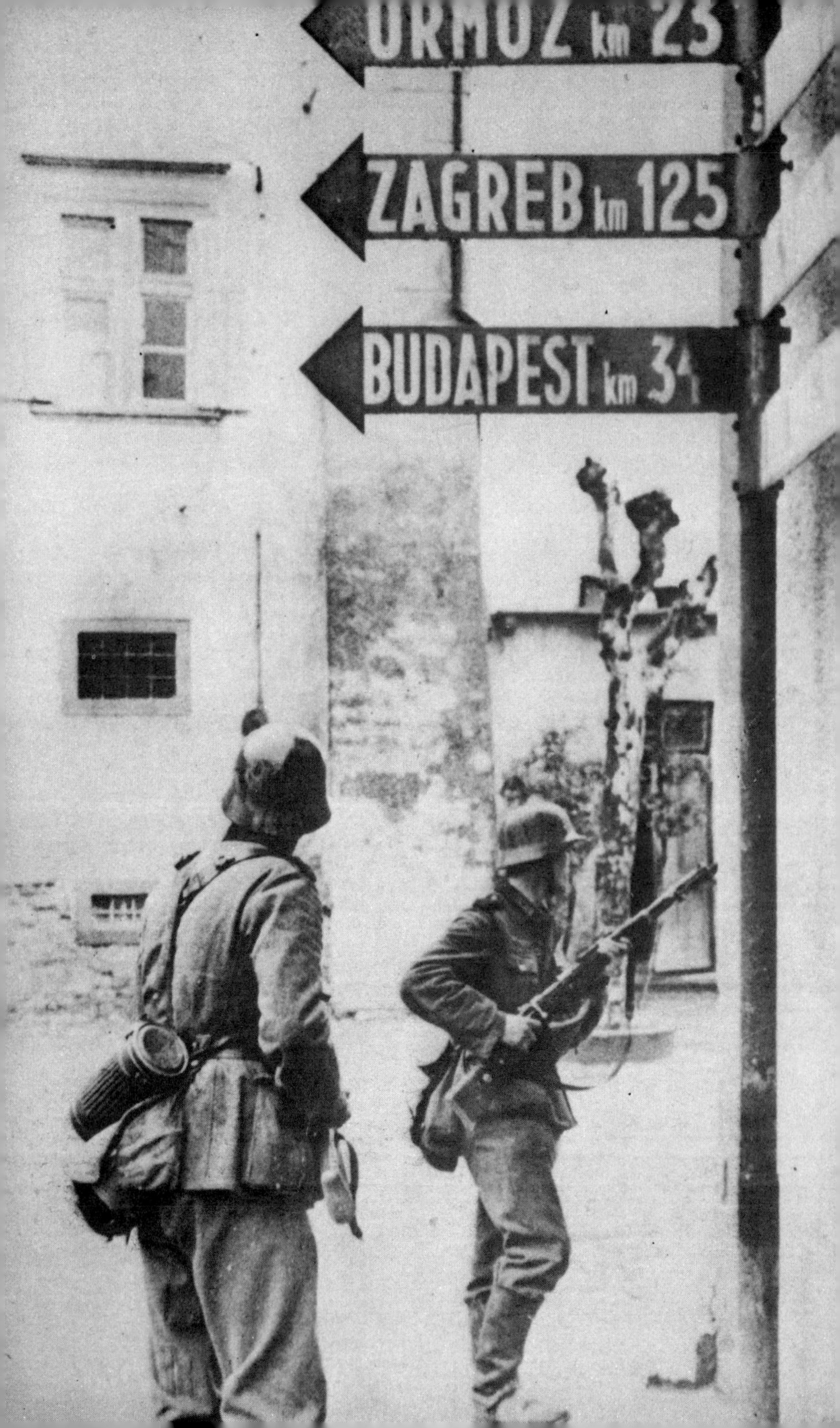
ORMOZ km 23
ZAGREB km 125
BUDAPEST km 34

ation 'academic,' as neither the Greeks nor the Turks would allow the RAF to use their airfields to bomb a country with which they were not at war, and the use of the Fleet Air Arm was out of the question. Furthermore any bombing of Rumania might prompt Hitler to occupy Bulgaria, putting the rest of the Balkans at risk: 'Until we are in a position to bomb the oil wells and refineries in such a fashion as to dislocate effectively Germany's oil supply for a lengthy period, it does not seem worthwhile embarking upon premature and inconclusive raids.'

Nevertheless, the project was still very much alive. The Air Staff argued in reply to the Foreign Office that 'strategic necessity and not political expediency' should dictate action against Rumanian oil, with the clear implication that violation of neutrality should be carried out if militarily necessary. Shortly before he left Bucharest the British Minister, Sir Reginald Hoare, advised that the Ploesti refineries were 'still relatively vulnerable' with few protective walls surrounding component units. Moreover, because of reduced winter exports, stocks were high (about 1,650,000 tons of refined products) and concentrated in a few places; and 'attacks on such points as Campina, Ploesti, Giurgiu and Constanta could simultaneously be directed against railway facilities, stocks and installations'. On 20th February pressure for action came from another quarter. The Special Operations Executive based on Cairo was about to launch a sabotage campaign against Rumanian oil and wanted an RAF 'token strike' in support. Anthony Eden, with the British Minister now out of Rumania, also emphasised the worth of attacking Constanta, Giurgiu and the Astra Romana refinery at Ploesti.

The Air Staff, however, was concerned not with the principle but the operation of such a plan. Rejecting the Special Operations Executive request, it explained that only nine Wellingtons and one squadron of Blenheim IVs were available in Greece and that, should Germany retaliate in kind, insufficient fighters existed to protect the Greek population. Already Sir Charles Portal had told Lord Hankey: 'I do not think that there is a chance in a hundred of the Greeks allowing us to use their country as a base of operations against Germany (sic) until they are at war with her', and on 25th February estimated that the Germans had 30-40 bombers capable of reaching Athens from Rumania and 100-120 dive bombers in Bulgaria able to attack Salonika. Furthermore, he was now afraid that air action might also provoke a ground invasion of Greece. Portal was therefore less than enthusiastic about the proposal; and the need for Greek co-operation, unlikely to be obtained, also cooled the Prime Minister's ardour. On 27th February Churchill informed Eden that, whatever the military opinion in the United Kingdom, 'the Greeks must clearly have the last word'.

Owing to obvious military and political difficulties, the concept was not actively pursued at this stage. The German invasion of Greece and Jugoslavia in April revived interest. On the 15th it was officially hoped that bombing of Rumania would commence as soon as possible, but the collapse of Greek resistance and the withdrawal of British forces from the mainland soon made an air attack impossible. Consequently, in view of post-war developments, a Foreign Office note of 25th April is of interest: 'We have recently been trying to interest the Russians in the possibility of starting some sort of revolutionary movement in Rumania with the object of securing her withdrawal from the war'. At this time neither the USSR nor Britain was at war with Rumania.

Invasion of Yugoslavia; German infantry engages in mopping up operations

Halpro: failure of a mission

Once Operation Barbarossa had brought the USSR into the war in June 1941 the Red Air Force carried out a few desultory raids on Rumania. In one of these, during the first week in July, two tankers were damaged in Constanta harbour and in others Bucharest and Ploesti received some attention. On 14th July six Russian aircraft attacked Unirea Orion from 2-3,000 feet at dusk and reputedly destroyed eighteen tanks, put the refinery out of action for four months and caused over one million dollars worth of damage. News of the Russian attacks prompted Lord Hankey to address 'a final appeal' to the British Chiefs of Staff for vigorous action against synthetic plants in Germany, but, with the main British bases now in North Africa, no realistic operations could be planned by the RAF against Rumania.

On 1st January 1942, however, the British again reviewed the situation. Ploesti was 380 miles from Sebastopol and 650 from Yekaterinodar in the USSR. From Cyrenaica to Yekaterinodar via Ploesti was 1,500 miles, so with Russian co-operation an air assault might be launched. During the Rumanian winter 30-40 degrees Fahrenheit of frost was normal and up to 60 degrees possible, therefore damage to houses as well as refineries could prove profitable. An average of two months was necessary to repair fully a bombed plant, with distillation units needing six weeks to three months, cracking units three to four months and boiler houses one to two months. With four-engined Liberators now at their disposal (bought as a commercial proposition before the

USA entered the war), the British might reduce Rumanian oil production from nine million to one million tons per year. Using 500-lb bombs and flying ninety sorties a month, one squadron of these heavy bombers would take seventeen months to achieve this objective, but two squadrons could succeed in little over five months.

However, the defences around Ploesti were known to be strong. Eight operational airfields were situated within 145km of the town; an inner belt of defences existed up to 8km and an outer ring up to 45km from its centre. The calibre of the defensive weapons increased from machine-guns near the refineries to heavy anti-aircraft guns in the outer ring, the latter manned by Germans after November 1941. Double brick walls with cement filling the intervening space had been erected around sensitive units: at Astra Romana these were up to 7m high with a base width of 1.3m tapering to 30cm at the top; those at Unirea Orion were 70cm at the base, 14cm at the top, with reinforcing brick pylons added every 5m along the wall. Many of the installations were also camouflaged (the fractionating tower at Dacia Romana being painted 'dirty green') and two dummy Ploestis were known to exist. One was 13km north-west, the other at Albesti, 12km east of Ploesti proper. The latter was an imitation town with refineries laid out in a contour of lights about one metre

German troops advance during Operation Barbarossa, which initiated the Russian attacks on Rumanian installations

above the ground and containing a small amount of oil which was fired during an attack. Primarily for the benefit of night bombers, on one occasion it deceived the Russians.

In February 1942 an RAF appreciation noted that the distance from Cyprus to Ploesti was only 700 miles, provided Turkish airspace was violated. If however this was politically unacceptable and Cyrenaica (El Adem being 900 miles from Ploesti) had to be used, Stirlings, Manchesters and Halifaxes would have insufficient range unless they were allowed to land and refuel in the USSR. The Liberator was the only aircraft able to fly to Ploesti and back, but there were only two RAF Liberator squadrons in the Middle East, which were not enough for an effective strike.

Two months later the project was examined yet again. The Ministry of Economic Warfare estimated that six of the Ploesti refineries achieved four million tons of refined production per year and that, in view of German commitment to the Russian campaign, decisive results could be gained if these were put out of action for three months. Headquarters RAF Middle East (HQ RAF ME) was asked by the Air Ministry: 'What force would be required and what is the possibility of achieving the object by one repeat one surprise low level day attack by heavy bombers carrying SAP bombs to be aimed at refinery power houses?' The Air Ministry added that the use of Beaufighters with AP incendiary cannon shells was being considered against distillation and cracking plants. HQ RAF ME was also required to estimate the possible success of a high-altitude night attack 'bearing in mind the difficulties of target location and anti-aircraft defences,' to comment upon the possibility of Russian co-operation and to examine the feasibility of a raid by 500 paratroops.

The reply on 26th April was not encouraging. Neutralisation of Ploesti's facilities for three months

could better be conducted through London and that Russian aircraft were probably incapable of effective action from their present bases. An assessment two days later noted that twelve airfields on Cyprus had long runways (five of them metalled), that Nicosia to Ploesti (over Turkey) was 850 miles, Krasnova to Ploesti 680 miles and Fuka (Egypt) to Ploesti 1,040 miles (avoiding neutral territory). It added that the Liberator II had an operational range of 1,820 miles and a cruising speed of 180mph at 15,000 feet in Middle East conditions.

In the third week of May the Air Ministry again raised the possibility of paratroop action. Quoting Mr Berthould, an oil expert, it argued that 30–40 paratroops could fire three or four pressure wells in the Tintea field which would not be extinguished for six months: during that period 10,000 tons of crude oil per well would be lost to the enemy. The possibility of combining a bombing attack against the Ploesti refineries with paratroop action on the Tintea oilfields ought therefore to be considered. HQ RAF ME replied promptly and critically. The paratroop raid might conceivably just prove profitable, but an engineer, Mr Glyn-Jones, had consulted technicians in Iraq and they concluded that, with modern methods, the Germans could extinguish a fire in one pressure well in a single day at the outside, though up to five days might be necessary to deal with four or five simultaneous fires. Furthermore, for safety purposes a minimum of wells were probably in use – at Kirkuk only five out of fifty were currently operational. The Air Ministry's equally sharp reply was that Major Boaden and Mr Forster, both experienced refinery managers, should be consulted forthwith and Captain Fitzroy Maclean asked to comment upon the use of

was not possible from Middle East bases and the chance of a successful low-level attack through flak and balloons was considered 'negligible'. HQ RAF ME emphasised that fifteen or sixteen power houses would have to be 'destroyed not damaged' and that 'the excess power available is probably 50 per cent above normal needs'. A day attack via the Aegean Sea, overflying Turkey, was thought to be 'hazardous' due to enemy RDF cover and needed a minimum of eight heavy bomber squadrons with 250-lb and 500-lb GP and incendiaries, not SAP bombs: a night attack against Astra Romana, with the possibility of inaccurate bombs falling on four other refineries, would be preferable. 'Direct attack by 500 paratroops extremely hazardous and would require large numbers of transport aircraft probably at the expense of bombing effort: infiltration by small parties of saboteurs probably more effective,' the reply continued. HQ RAF ME thought negotiations with the USSR

paratroops. HQ RAF ME eventually did agree that 'there is a chance technically speaking of achieving this object,' but pleaded that no personnel were available for a paratroop drop at present. This lack of enthusiasm from Cairo for an airborne operation followed hard upon an earlier assertion that the RAF was incapable of bombing Ploesti from the Middle East.

In fact no RAF consideration of action against Ploesti in 1942 could be carried out without reference to the USA, which had shown interest in the Rumanian oil industry virtually as soon as it entered the war. Within a month of the attack on Pearl Harbor the Americans had produced a feasibility study concerning an attack on Ploesti. Even before the Lend-Lease Act of March 1941, early P-40 fighter models had been acquired by the RAF in the Middle East and many USAAF personnel had found their way to the Nile Delta as advisers or maintenance men. Most of these men and machines had flown fromTakoradi

in West Africa via a series of temporary staging posts, with romantically improbable names like Maiduguri, Fort Lamy, Ati, El Geneina and El Obeid and established in all manner of unlikely places, over hills, deserts and swamps across the whole breadth of the continent to Khartoum, then up to bases in the Nile Delta. First used in September 1940 this route, officially the West African Reinforcement Route, reached a peak delivery figure of 1,455 new aircraft from May to December 1942.

During June 1941 the Takoradi route was linked with the USA by flying aircraft from American factories to Florida, then on to the Antilles, Natal on the Atlantic coast of Brazil, across the Atlantic to Gambia and Sierra Leone or Liberia, and ultimately to Takoradi in the Gold Coast territory. In September 1941 the US North African Military Mission was created and a month later Brigadier-General Russel L Maxwell was instructed to organise and operate supply, maintenance and training facilities for British and other friendly forces in the area. Meanwhile Americans were flying lend-lease aircraft into Egypt and gaining valuable experience in Middle East conditions. Once the USA was at war with the Axis powers Maxwell's role changed from advice and assistance to deployment of American resources.

Forward plans considered the possibility of American bombers (even B-29 Superfortresses, not yet in service) ultimately operating out of Egypt against southern Europe to supplement action from Britain. But at the Arcadia Conference in Decem-

US army and airforce personnel arrive to begin construction of an advanced base in the Western Desert

r 1941 between British and American
presentatives in Washington no
rge commitment of American per-
nnel to the area was immediately
reseen. However with the loss of
uam and Wake islands in the same
onth, it was decided to reinforce the
hilippines via the Middle East, Iran,
dia and Burma, as the route by way
Hawaii and Australia was not yet
lly operational. This entailed a
inforcement of American personnel
d facilities in the Middle East,
hich became still more important
a staging post once Major-General
wis H Brereton's Tenth Air Force
as established in India during
arch 1942.

With American servicemen now
ysically committed to the Middle
st in some strength, Britain was
xious to involve the USAAF more
lly in operations. In January 1942
sk Force Cairo, which aimed at
quiring two fighter groups within
x months, was set up on paper,
ough the USA opposed allocation
a bombardment group to its
rength on the grounds that this
uld have to come from aircraft
stined for the campaign against
ermany from the United Kingdom.
wever by March it had been agreed
at if Britain deployed American-
ilt aircraft from its own supply in
e theatre, the USAAF would man
em. Thus a strength of five groups
as foreseen at some future date.
lthough by Spring 1942 no strong
merican operational commitment to
attack on Ploesti had been estab-
hed, a planning interest had been
own and USAAF involvement in
e Middle East suggested possible
tion later.

In fact, attack on industrial targets
as very much in line with USAAF
mbing policy. Throughout the years
tween the First and Second World
ars theorists like Guilio Douhet

Between the wars Sir Hugh Trenchard
(*Above*) and General William Mitchell
(*Below*) both emphasised the need to
develop a heavy bomber

r Chief Marshal Sir Arthur Tedder,
ft, and Major-General Lewis H
ereton

and experienced airmen like Sir Hugh (later Lord) Trenchard in Britain and William Mitchell in the USA had emphasised the need to develop heavy bombers. Specifically the doctrine of strategic bombing – striking at the source of an enemy's power in his homeland – had evolved from limited experience in the First World War and the arguments of such protaganists of air power. The precise targets for a strategic bombing campaign – cities, military installations or factories – were not universally agreed. But the American position was clear. The USA firmly held that only industrial targets connected with the war effort should be attacked. Hence, on 1st September 1939, the day war broke out in Europe President Roosevelt appealed to all belligerents not to indulge in unrestricted air warfare, which might involve non-military targets and personnel. This policy

was summarised early in the war I General H H Arnold, Chief of the U Army Air Forces: 'The primary fun tion of bombardment is to destrc vital enemy facilities, factories etc The aim of the American heav bombers therefore was precisic bombing against important industri targets within the enemy's homelan

The Rumanian oil industry, and particular the refineries at Ploest were thus bound to attract USAA attention in the course of time. Tl British had already pointed out th: only the Liberator (the British nan for the B-24) could complete a rour trip to Ploesti from North Africa bases. This aircraft had been deve oped comparatively recently. Tl contract for a prototype, with spec fications of 300mph, 3,000 mile rang and 35,000-foot ceiling had bee awarded to the Consolidated Aircra Corporation in March 1939, but tl

B-24 did not fly until 29th December 1939. Characterised by a high-aspect ratio wing with the Davis high-lift aerofoil, the aircraft experienced less drag than machines of a more conventional design. Twin fins in the tail section aimed to give more accuracy in precision bombing, though in many respects this slab-like aircraft was difficult to handle. The central bomb-bay, divided into front and rear compartments, was designed to carry 8000 lbs of bombs, but the XB-24, despite its four 1,200hp Pratt and Whitney engines, could only reach 273mph and its armament consisted of only three hand-held .3 calibre machine-guns forward and twin .3s in the tail. Such was the pressure for heavy bombers in addition to the B-17 (Flying Fortresses) already in service that the Army Air Corps placed an order for thirty-six B-24s despite the aircraft's recognised drawbacks. In

The Consolidated XB-24

addition Britain ordered 164 and France 120, the latter being added to the British order when France fell.

The first British model (the LB-30A, which the RAF named 'Liberator') flew on 17th January 1941. Six months later the USAAF received its first operational B-24A, which had six. 50s plus twin .3 machine-guns in the tail. The Liberator II appeared in the Middle East in November 1941, but this was a special RAF type which did not go into active service with the USAAF: 139, armed with ten .303 machine-guns, were obtained by Britain. Meanwhile, in the USA many design changes had taken place and the first Liberator model to reach USAAF units for bombing, as opposed to reconnaissance purposes, was the B-24D. It had ten .50 machine-guns, a maximum bomb load of 8,000 lbs and a

Lieutenant-General H H Arnold, Chief of the US Army Air Forces

US Army Chief of Staff, General George C Marshall

fuel capacity boosted by auxiliary self-sealing tanks in the outer wings to 3,009 Imperial (3,614 American) gallons, plus space for further tanks in the bomb-bay. Later versions of the B-24D had a retractable Briggs-Sperry electrically-operated ball turret aft of the bomb-bay, though this created more drag and reduced the maximum speed below the theoretical 303mph at 25,000 feet. Overall the standard B-24D, with a wing span of 110 feet, was 66 feet-4 inches long and 18 feet high, cruised economically at 200mph, had a ceiling of 28,000 feet and a maximum range of 2,300 miles. The armament of different versions of the B-24D varied between six and eleven .50 machine-guns and the crew numbered either nine or ten. The portly appearance of the fuselage earned the B-24 the nick-name of 'Pregnant Cow' from Flying Fortress men and, due to instability in certain circumstances, 'Banana Boat' from its own crews.

As a general purpose aircraft the

B-24 fulfilled a number of roles (reco naissance, ferrying, bombing) an Lewis H Brereton, who was to com mand the Ninth Air Force engaged i the 1943 Ploesti raid, considered it magnificent hunk of bomber'. Cur ously, however, Jacob E Smart, wh helped to plan that low-level attack thought it a poor aircraft for this typ of mission: 'Of all the world's ai craft there is probably none les suited to ground strafing than th B-24. It is relatively slow . . . and t the man on the ground it appears tha it can be knocked down with a rock His conclusion was to prove terr fyingly accurate on 1st August 1943.

In the meantime, chance had mad a number of USAAF B-24s available t attack Ploesti in mid-1942. Early i January the AAF Plans Division i Washington considered a conclusio by Colonel Bonner F Fellers, Amer can Military Attaché in Cairo, tha Ploesti was vulnerable to attack b heavy bombers, and towards the en of that month Harry L Hopkins

President Roosevelt's adviser, asked General Arnold whether such an air attack would be possible. Arnold replied that, although losses might be very high, B-24s from Britain could reach Budapest in Hungary. Ploesti was beyond their range and no American heavy bombers could be spared for the Middle East to attack from there. Two months later Fellers returned to the subject by emphasising that the Rumanian oil industry was 'within easy reach' of American bombers from Egypt and that Air Chief Marshal Sir Arthur Tedder, RAF Air Officer Commanding-in-Chief Middle East, was willing to provide fuel, bombs, ammunition and maintenance facilities. Fellers thought Rumanian oil constituted 'by far the most decisive objective . . . the strategic target of the war' and urged that an American task force should be sent to the Middle East to make a positive contribution in that theatre.

At this time, following Lieutenant-Colonel James H Doolittle's carrier-borne attack on Tokio from *Enterprise* and *Hornet* in April, it was planned to fly twenty-four B-24s under the command of Colonel A Halverson to China to carry out a land-based attack on Japan from the west. By mid-May this project began to look dubious as Japanese forces driving westwards threatened to engulf the Chenkiang airfields from which the Halverson Project (Halpro) aircraft intended to attack. On 15th May 1942 a Plans Division evaluation concluded that a mission against Ploesti was the best means of assisting the USSR, now faced with a resumption of the German advance previously halted by winter conditions. On that day the Assistant Chief of Air Staff, Plans, recommended that the Halpro force be used against Ploesti because of the uncertain military position in China. Next day the RAF delegation (RAFDEL) in Washington signalled that General George C Marshall, US Army Chief of Staff, had announced his intention of advising the President

that the B-24s intended for China and ready to leave the USA, should 'now be employed for surprise operations from the Middle East against oil refineries at Ploesti'. Marshall wanted to attack as soon as possible and was anxious to use Aleppo in Syria as a base. RAFDEL, noting that the RAF had considerable data available from previous study of such a project, believed that two American heavy groups could be accommodated in the Middle East, and favoured operations from the Nile Delta or the Western Desert to prevent violation of Turkish air space. The Air Ministry in London immediately replied instructing the Washington delegation to welcome Marshall's plan, adding that it was 'very desirable to get US Air Forces established in Middle East and this an excellent pretext'. The Air Ministry recorded an HQ RAF ME estimate that a minimum of eight squadrons (128 aircraft) would be necessary for a surprise daylight attack and then revived another favourite concept: 'There are possibilities in a surprise paratroop attack for which these aircraft might be used'.

President Roosevelt approved Marshall's suggestion and logistic requirements were quickly forwarded to London. Halpro B-24s were capable of a 'still air range' of 3,000 miles and with an anticipated 58,000 lbs gross weight would require 3,000 gallons of fuel per aircraft. In addition, 3,000 rounds of .50 ammunition and a 6,000-lb bomb load per aircraft per sortie must be provided for. On 17th May RAFDEL informed London that twenty-three B-24s could be anticipated at Khartoum in the Sudan via Central America, Brazil and the Takoradi route on about 28th May. Colonel Halverson intended to lead the formation personally, which would consist of three echelons of seven, eight and eight and depart from the USA on 22nd May, the same day that an advance party of Colonel Craw, Major Zuckerman and Major Williams arrived in Cairo. The air-

Field-Marshal Sir John Dill

craft would remain at Khartoum for security reasons, though ultimate forward movement to Aleppo or Mosul (Iraq) was planned. Two days later RAFDEL signalled: 'US authorities request rigid censorship regarding preparations for operation and no subsequent publicity'.

The impending arrival of Halpro aircraft at Wadi Seidna, Khartoum, prompted a British request that they be used to help protect vital convoys sailing to relieve the beleaguered island of Malta. Early in June Field-Marshal Sir John Dill, Head of the British Joint Staff Mission in Washington, reported that Marshall believed use of the B-24s in support of a Malta convoy would reveal their presence in the Middle East – which showed a touching faith in Egyptian security. Dill advised that further pressure for use of the bombers in this role might cause resentment, but commented that 'Americans attach a very exaggerated value to the Halpro operation which incidentally I think

originated with the President'. According to Dill, General Marshall thought 'if successfully accomplished this mission would have a major effect on the whole war' and if surprise were achieved it 'would have better than an even chance to succeed'.

Winston Churchill, undeterred by Dill, drafted a personal appeal to President Roosevelt for use of Halpro aircraft to prevent the surrender of Malta and its 30,000 troops, emphasising that the enemy must already know of Halverson's arrival at Khartoum. In fact Churchill did not send this message although further representations were made to Marshall who reluctantly agreed that the planes might be used, but only if the Italian fleet ventured into the Mediterranean. With this the British Prime Minister had to be content. By 7th June three Halpro aircraft were already at Fayid airfield on the western shore of the Great Bitter Lake in Egypt and sixteen more were expected from Khartoum on the morrow, rounding off a flight from the USA of nearly 4,000 miles. En route the aircraft had survived a cyclone and a landing by one B-24 at the remote outpost of El Fasher to refuel. Shortly afterwards HQ RAF ME killed lingering hopes of an immediate paratroop drop, by revealing that the only suitable personnel were concerned with another mission until 22nd June. Thereafter the next possible moon period would be 7th July. As this would leave no time to train the men to jump from B-24s in a strange country, August was considered the earliest practicable time for such an operation. Colonel Halverson was willing to co-operate and it was therefore thought better to wait until the later date to avoid possible confusion due to insufficient training. HQ RAF ME believed that a previous bombing attack on the refineries at Ploesti would not prejudice this airborne project, but rather assist it as the Rumanians would not think the oilfields in danger.

Arrangements therefore were made for Colonel Halverson's force to bomb the Astra Romana refinery at Ploesti at dawn on 12th June 1942, with the possibility that in August the B-24s would return with paratroops to sabotage the Tintea oil wells. The RAF AOC-in-C ME, Air Chief Marshal Tedder, complained after the mission that the 'force did not operate under my orders and from the moment of arrival Colonel Halverson was most unwilling to accept any operational advice or instruction'. Undoubtedly Halverson did upset RAF officers in Egypt, but he firmly believed that this must be an exclusively American mission, as a matter of national pride. For, with the exception of Doolittle's effort in the Far East, no independent USAAF bombing mission had yet been carried out on enemy territory. To allow a dawn attack, the Halpro aircraft left Fayid between 2230 and 2300 hours on 11th June. Officially the thirteen which took off (the maximum available due to maintenance problems), following an RAF plan prepared by 205 Group, were to proceed individually northwards over the eastern Mediterranean and rendezvous shortly after dawn near Constanta on the western shore of the Black Sea for a combined bombing attack. The outward flight would be at 30,000 feet, with a descent after the rendezvous to a bombing height of 10-12,000 feet. From Constanta the aircraft were to fly up the oil pipe-line to the Danube on its northward course to Galatz, pick up its tributary the Ialomita and in turn the river Teleajen until Ploesti was reached. The B-24s would return to Fayid and on both legs of their 2,600 mile flight skirt Turkey to the west to avoid violating her neutral airspace.

This was agreed, and the need to circumvent Turkey emphasised, at a general briefing on 11th June. But immediately after this Halverson called another briefing, from which RAF personnel were excluded. It then emerged that Halverson proposed to make for Habbaniyeh airfield in Iraq after the attack, and he could not be persuaded otherwise. Tedder bitterly commented: 'I suspect that he had no intention of respecting Turkish neutrality despite my injunctions to the contrary,' for the British also believed that at the private briefing Halverson decided to make straight for Constanta on the outward journey by flying over, not round, Turkey. It further appeared that, although the aircraft took off singly as planned, no arrangements for a rendezvous had been made and no procedure for proper target identification laid down.

Officially all thirteen aircraft 'reached the objective' with 'a majority of the aircraft bombing from below the clouds', 'about ten' hitting Astra Romana, one Constanta and the remaining two 'unidentified targets'. In the course of the raid 'a few fighter aircraft, fairly heavy anti-aircraft artillery, and a balloon barrage' were encountered and 'at least one Me-109 was destroyed'. But an RAF assessment dated 14th June concluded otherwise: 'The general impression is that the majority of aircraft jettisoned their bombs either on the ETA (estimated time of arrival over the target) from above the clouds (about 16,000 feet) or on breaking cloud. It is highly improbable that any damage has been done'.

In fact one aircraft dropped its bombs over Constanta harbour, then turned back with mechanical trouble; the other twelve did not rendezvous, but proceeded individually to where they thought the target was. Here each ejected 4,000 lbs of bombs, some through cloud of 10,000 feet minimum altitude, with no visible sighting of the target. The USAAF quoted an 'unconfirmed report' that 'an (unspecified) oil depot at Ploesti was destroyed, one bomb fell in the woods, another hit a railway station, while several fell on Constanta without doing much damage'; Rumanian and German sources affected not to notice the intrusion. *The Times* in

London a week later printed a report from its Ankara correspondent that 'so far as can be ascertained the raid was most successful. All the stores, refineries and other installations at Ploesti were hit and set on fire'. Almost certainly this particular fairytale was based upon information from American flyers, who had been interned after landing in Turkey. For only four aircraft (including Halverson's) reached Habbaniyeh after twelve hours in the air, three landed elsewhere in Iraq (at Ramadi, Mosul and Deir ez Zor), two at Aleppo in Syria and four in Turkey (one on two engines near Ada Bazaar and three at Ankara civil airport). The British Naval Attaché in Ankara reported that the latter three were all virtually out of fuel and 'on getting out of the planes the pilots produced a notebook with the telephone numbers of the British and American attachés,' which he considered 'looked fishy'. He added that apparently Ploesti was surrounded by heavy anti-aircraft

defences and that German fighter had pursued the B-24s until Turkis guns on the European side of the Bos phurus Straits had opened up an forced them to turn back into Bul garia. The four aircraft and thirty seven crew members were interned i Turkey. Before all the men were a length repatriated, one entire cre escaped to Cyprus in their aircraft which following official protests from Ankara was returned to Turkey with out them. At one stage a plan t exchange one B-24 for two Baltimore was put forward but never seriousl pursued. The aircraft were thus ac quired by the Turkish Air Force an the Halpro mission to Ploesti effec tively lost four ·out of thirtee Liberators.

The whole disappointing episode for nothing did in fact hit the Astr Romana refinery, caused Tedder t reach a hasty, sweeping and unjus conclusion: 'This fiasco confirms ou first impression that the standar of training of the crews in this forc

s such as to render them practically
seless for any purpose'. After
'edder's report and comments, the
3ritish Air Ministry pithily drew
ttention to the Americans' previous
emand for no publicity and added:
Propose comply this request es-
ecially in view pathetic results
btained'.

Halverson's remaining aircraft and
rews stayed on in Egypt to do valu-
ble work in the Mediterranean and
oin with the Ninth Bombardment
quadron as a 'Provisional Bombard-
ent Group,' later to become the
76th Bombardment Group which re-
isited Ploesti after nearly fourteen
ore months. Colonel Halverson him-
elf soon returned to the USA, pos-
ibly as a result of British pressure.
ertainly Tedder continued to agitate
bout his deviation from the RAF
lan of attack. Three days after the
iission he wrote to the Air Ministry
gain: 'I saw Colonel Halverson and
thers of the party and personally
istructed him that he was not on any

account to overfly Turkey'. Early in
1943, however, an RAF summary of
previous year's events in the Middle
East indirectly justified Halverson's
decision and obliquely criticised the
RAF plan given to him. It pointed out
that the direct round trip Fayid to
Ploesti was 2,000 miles. A diversion
round the western border of European
Turkey both ways would have brought
the B-24s dangerously close to their
maximum operational range and left
very little margin for error or de-
creased performance due to mechanical malfunction or damage from
enemy action. Furthermore thorough
dispersal of the B-24s was not possible
at Fayid, which might suffer a retalia-
tory enemy air strike after their
return. With these factors in mind
the decision was taken to fly to
Habbaniyeh, the summary concluded.

Whatever the truth of this particular matter, and undoubtedly a clash
of personality between Halverson and
Tedder plus American insistence upon
secrecy has not assisted clarification,
it is evident that little, if any, important damage was achieved in the
Ploesti area. General Eisenhower
commented that the raid 'did something to dispel the illusion that a few
big planes could win a war'; but this
Halpro attack did prove the long
range capability of the B-24 in action.
Failure of the mission determined
that any future USAAF venture of a
similar nature would be carried out by
a very much larger force and be flown
entirely in daylight. Unfortunately
the enemy also benefited from the
experience. He was alerted to the
possibility of air attack on Rumania
from Africa, hitherto thought incon-
ceivable, and strengthened his defences accordingly.

Thus both sides drew conclusions
from the events of 11th-12th June 1942,
which ensured a more dramatic and
destructive round of the contest the
following year.

Ploesti: priority target

After Halverson's failure Rumanian oil remained an object of special importance for both sides in the war. In November 1942, with the German Sixth Army under General von Paulus already in peril at Stalingrad, Colonel-General Jodl, Wehrmacht Chief of Staff, commented that 'no success gained by the enemy there (the eastern front) can be directly disastrous unless we should lose the Rumanian oilfields'. A month earlier a meeting of the *Zentrung Planung* had been told that all Wehrmacht reserves of motor gasoline were exhausted. The position was therefore critical, although monthly syntheti production had risen by 60,000 tons t a total 260,000 tons during 1942 and new plant had come into operation a Breux in Czechoslovakia. So desperat was the need for more oil that, befor German forces crossed the Don rive in Summer 1942 to strike into Cau casia, specially-trained men had bee assembled to repair damage which th retreating Russians were expected t cause to their refineries. Seventy-fiv drilling rigs were also collected t exploit the 250,000 tons of oil antici pated from Maikop during the firs year of German occupation. Yet, a

Below left and above: Rumanian oil is transferred from railway tankers for transportation to the German front line. *Below:* German infantry and tank assault during the advance into Caucasia

the same time, because of her dependence upon neutral countries for supplies of raw materials and certain manufactured goods (such as anti-friction bearings), Germany agreed to allow Sweden to import 2,000 tons of Rumanian oil per month; and on another occasion she undertook herself to supply oil to Switzerland.

In fact, by 1942 Rumania was not providing Germany's needs satisfactorily. From Rumania's total oil exports of 4,494,762 tons in 1938 Germany took 999,240: by 1941 these figures were respectively 4,072,306 and 2,919,580 and a year later 3,373,542 and 2,191,659. One factor contributing to this decline was the rise in Rumanian domestic consumption from 1,811,000 to 2,098,000 tons between 1941 and 1942. Another reason was that, although crude oil output rose during the same period from 5,577,000 to 5,665,000 tons, refinery production dropped from 5,255,000 to 5,237,000 tons. No Allied action was responsible for this.

Nonetheless, these variations did not vitally reduce the importance of Rumanian oil supplies for Germany. Late in 1942 the RAF emphasised that Rumania produced 5,200,000 tons of crude oil per year (a slight underestimate), 80 per cent of which was dealt with by six refineries in the Ploesti area: these included the only paraffin wax and many of the main lubricating oil refineries of the country. At this time also American sources drew attention to the location of twenty Rumanian oilfields in an area sixty miles long and ten miles wide just north of Ploesti. In this region the wells averaged one every ten acres, though a density of eight or ten per ten acres did exist in places. Most of the extracted crude oil was stored in field tanks, then carried via pipe or railway tank car to the refineries, but 'neither the oil wells themselves nor the storage tanks were considered profitable targets for aerial bombardment'. The refineries were thought much more important and easier to locate: those near

Ploesti produced 85 per cent of Rumania's refined petroleum and possessed almost 95 per cent of her cracking capacity.

In Spring 1943, with memories of June 1942 fading and possibly fired with enthusiasm at early American bombing successes over Europe, pressure began to mount for another attack on Ploesti. In reply to an Allied Combined Chiefs of Staff (CCS) instruction, on 8th March 1943 the Committee of Operations Analysts in Washington listed petroleum as the third most important enemy target, after the fighter industry and ball-bearings. Its sub-committee on the Axis Oil Industry reported that two-third of Axis oil supplies came from crude oil (60 per cent of which derived from the Ploesti area), the remaining one-third from synthetic plants in Germany. Effective action against the thirteen most import synthetic plants would therefore eliminate one quarter of Germany's available petrol resources, including two-thirds of her existing production of aviation fuel. Stocks could not alleviate the full effect of such an assault for more than four months. If, in addition, some twenty-six refineries could be destroyed total petroleum supplies would be cut by 90 per cent. A month later, in Britain, the Assistant Chief of the Air Staff stated: 'There has been a tendency for Axis oil stocks to increase recently' and attempted to goad his masters into positive action by adding that 'the situation may not therefore be as critical as we should like it to be'.

Partly as a result of economic arguments, in the Pointblank Plan for bomber action against Axis targets approved by the CCS on 14th May 1943 oil was put fourth on the list of principal objectives. The planners commented that refinery and synthetic oil products were now 'barely adequate to supply the life-blood which is vital to the German war machine' and that the enemy position had been made 'more critical' by his failure to

The Russian counterattack at Kursk

ecure the Russian supplies in Cau-
asia. They considered that: 'If
Ploesti refineries, which process 35 per
ent of current refinery oil production
available to the Axis, be destroyed,
nd the synthetic oil plants in Germany which process an additional
3 per cent are also destroyed, the
esulting disruption will have a
disastrous effect upon the supply of
nished oil products available to the
Axis'. On 1st July Mr Berthoud, of
he British Ministry of Fuel and
Power, estimated that current Axis
annual oil production of all types
mounted to 17,000,000 tons, of which
0 per cent came from the Ploesti area.
hortly afterwards the American
ommittee on Axis oil considered that
otal German stocks at the beginning
f the year were 5,000,000 tons, though
he British put them at only 3,000,000;
ubsequent information revealed that
oth these figures were too high. The
pening of the massive German panzer
ffensive at Kursk in the first week of
uly, with its obvious debilitating

effect on enemy stocks, underlined
the damage which a successful
attack on Ploesti could achieve.

One important consideration to be
faced was the strength of enemy
defences around the town, which increased considerably after mid-1942.
During the Second World War the
Germans failed to develop an efficient
medium calibre (50–70mm) anti-aircraft gun, but did produce good light
(20–40mm) and heavy weapons. The
aim of the former was the maximum
volume of fire to force aircraft high
and therefore hopefully to bomb less
accurately. The 20mm Flak 30 which
originally came into service in 1935
with an effective rate of fire of 120 rpm
(rounds per minute) and a ceiling of
6,630 feet was the basis for all 20mm
models early in the war. 20mm Flak 38
appeared in 1940. Firing the same
range of 3.6–5.2-ounce AP or HE shells,
with an improved sight and redesigned
breech mechanism, it was capable of

69

bove: German 88mm Flak 36 in action. *Left:* The German 128mm Flak 40.
elow: The standard 88mm anti-aircraft gun in use in its anti-tank role

480rpm. Both Flak 30 and Flak 38 remained in service but, in an attempt to simplify the mechanism, an open-ring replaced the computer sight in 1941. In the same year a quadruple version of Flak 38 (20mm Flakvierling 38) was introduced with the four barrels effectively firing 800rpm. The 37mm Flak 18 light anti-aircraft weapon also actively appeared in 1935, with a maximum ceiling of 15,750 feet and a practical capability of 80rpm. A later model, 37mm Flak 36, became the standard gun of this calibre during the war, but a twin-barrelled version, 37mm Flakzwilling 43, was not successful.

At the outbreak of war in 1939 Germany had heavy anti-aircraft artillery based upon 88mm and 105mm guns, with the 128mm about to go into production: a planned 150mm was never actually developed. 88mm Flak 18 first appeared in 1932 and a later version, 88mm Flak 36, with a three section barrel, went into mass production five years later. In 1939 came 88mm Flak 37 with a modified transmission system, which remained the basic 88mm anti-aircraft weapon until 1943. Capable of 15–20rpm and an effective ceiling of 26,250 feet (theoretically 34,770), it could reach the height flown by any Allied bomber with 20-lb 1-oz – 21-lb ½-oz HE or AP shells.

The 105mm weapon was conceived in 1933 to deal with aircraft which might in future fly above the 88mm's effective ceiling, and 105mm Flak 38 was developed three years later. With a modified transmission system it became 105mm Flak 39 in 1939: both models fired a 34-lb 5-oz shell at 10 – 15rpm, theoretically to a height of 42,000 feet. 128mm Flak 40 fired a 62-lb 8-oz shell at 12rpm to a maximum height of 48,500 feet and its twin version, 128mm Flakzwilling 40, hopefully achieved 20 – 25rpm. But the 128mm guns were almost exclusively used to defend sensitive areas in Germany, often mounted on concrete flak towers. No 105mm nor 128mm guns

were at Ploesti in 1943, despite American aircrew claims to the contrary. But standard 20mm, 37mm and 88mm versions were there, plus some 20mm Flakvierling 38s. The presence many 88mm guns, so formidable ove 20,000 feet, was a strong reason fo carrying out a low-level attack o Ploesti in the hope that the light weapons would prove less destructiv

Fighters too formed a powerful pa of German air defences. In earl stages of the war the twin-engine Messerschmitt Me-110 had done val able service. But with a speed 288mph, some 60mph slower than th Spitfire, it was gradually withdraw to a night fighter role together wit other twin-engined aircraft like th Ju-88. The main day fighters from 19 onwards were the single-engine Messerschmitt Bf 109 and Focke-Wu Fw 190. The prototype of the forme designed at the Messerschmitt worl near Augsburg had first flown in 19 powered by an imported Rolls Roye Kestrel engine. The Me-109 (as it wa more generally known) saw actio during the Spanish Civil War ar within eighteen months of the sta of the Second World War the Luf waffe was flying the Me-109E versio Its armament varied: either four MG wing-mounted machine-guns or tw fuselage-mounted MG17s and tw wing cannon or four MG17s on th wings and a single 20mm canno mounted on the fuselage. With speed of 355mph at 12,000 feet and ceiling of 36,000 feet, its all-round pe formance roughly equalled that of th Hurricane. A later model, Me-109 with an improved engine performan giving a speed of 380mph became avai able in large numbers in mid-1941 western Europe (though not th Balkans). By the end of 1942 th Me-109G with heavier armament ar a theoretical speed of about 400mp was in service. The Fw 190, with i distinctive air-cooled radial engin was an even more formidable oppo ent for the heavy bombers. Four 20m cannon were mounted on its win and two 7.9mm machine-guns over the engine. Its speed was similar to that of the Me-109G and it too could operate with little reduction in performance at altitudes over 20,000 feet. Versions of the Me-109E, Me-109F and Fw 190A, which were in service in the Balkans in 1943, had a flight endurance time of ninety minutes.

The Germans did develop radar coverage, which early in the war was not always used to advantage – possibly because of Hitler's insistence that the Luftwaffe was a purely attacking force. Early Freya sets could give no altitude reading and had a range of only thirty-six miles, though this increased in 1942 to seventy-five miles. The air defence system had been made more efficient a year earlier by the addition of mobile Wurzburg sets able to plot accurately up to twenty-five miles and, shortly afterwards, so-called Giant Wurzburgs (due to their massive 23-foot reflectors), effective up to forty-five miles, became operational. Furthermore direction-finding equipment was ready to home on any unwary radio transmissions from aircraft or their bases.

When the Germans moved into Rumania and Bulgaria, they took their anti-aircraft weapons, aircraft and radars with them. Although the Balkans did not rank high on the priority list for equipment before 1943, nevertheless respectable defences around Ploesti were soon created and within their framework the Bulgarian and Rumanian airforces could not be entirely discounted. The former, like the Luftwaffe, had risen Phoenix-like from the 1918 ashes. Because Bulgaria supported the Central Powers in the First World War she was denied an air force by the Treaty of Neuilly. Although this treaty was not openly renounced until 1937, for nine years previously an airforce had been surreptitiously developed. The state aircraft works near Sofia produced the DAR-6A trainer, which together with twenty-four PZL P-24G single-seater fighters

purchased from Poland, formed the basis for the 1st Bulgarian Fighter Regiment (Orlek). In the late 1930s a rapid programme of expansion took place, with aircraft manufactured at home and purchased from abroad (delivery of fifty-four P-43s was underway when the Germans invaded Poland). At the outbreak of war the Bulgarian Air Force, an integral part of the army and commanded by General Ajranof, had eight regiments. When Bulgaria adhered to the Axis Tripartite Pact on 1st March 1941, its strength was augmented by nineteen Me-109Es and a collection of twin-engined Ju-86D, Ju-87B and Do-17M aircraft. Until Autumn 1943, however, the Bulgarian Air Force was in reality weak. It had acquired a few Luftwaffe advisers and instructors, but Germany's interest in the country largely evaporated once its bases had been successfully used by the Luftwaffe to subdue Greece in 1941. The Bulgarian lack of front-line aircraft was emphasised by the continuation in service of Letov S-328 and Avia B-534 biplanes – scarcely airworthy and of doubtful combat worth. The latter, equipped with four 7.7mm machine-guns, had a theoretical ceiling of 34,878 feet, but took five minutes to climb to 16,400 feet and with difficulty managed a speed of 230mph. Nevertheless the Bulgarians did have their Me-109s and for operational purposes came under the direction of the German *Luftflotte 4*.

The Rumanian Air Force was an altogether stronger body. Having declared for the victors Rumania did not lose her air arm for the First World War. In the inter-war period she reorganised her airforce, established training schools at Tecuciu and Bucharest, purchased British and French aircraft to supplement those she had confiscated from the defeated Germans and developed her own Regina Autonoma Industria Aeronautica Romana (IAR) aircraft production factory at Brasov. In 1939 the Rumanian Air Force with about 500

Above: One of the main day fighters from 1941 onwards, the Focke-Wulf Fw 190.
Below: The ME-109F, in service in the Balkans in 1943

Above: The Polish single-seater fighter PZL P-24, which formed the basis for the Bulgarian Fighter Regiment. *Below:* Pre-war Bulgarian pilots during training

aircraft and six commands (one being anti-aircraft artillery) was the strongest in the Balkans, even though many of its aircraft were obsolescent. The German invasion of Poland, however, proved something of a windfall. Ninety-three Polish machines, including thirty-eight P-7 and P-11 single seater fighters, arrived at Cherniovce airfield and were promptly acquired for local use. Britain and France sought to stiffen Rumanian resistance to German pressure early in 1940 by supplying aircraft like the Blenheim I and Hurricane IV, though in comparatively small numbers. Once Rumania signed the Tripartite Pact in November 1940, however, a Luftwaffe mission descended on Bucharest with a squadron of He-112B single-seater fighters (previously rejected for service in western Europe), forty Me-109Es and a squadron of He-111H-3 bombers. In preparation for the coming struggle against the USSR the Rumanian Air Force was administratively organised in accordance with Luftwaffe practice, whilst remaining officially autonomous under its own Under-Secretary of State for Air and Commanding-General responsible to the Chief of the General Staff. By 1943 the Rumanian Air Force consisted of some 13,000 men (including two brigades of anti-aircraft artillery) and about 700 aircraft, half of which were fighters. By now the IAR factory was manufacturing its version of the Italian SM-79B powered by Junkers Jumo 211F engines and Rumanian IAR 80 fighters and IAR 81 fighter-bombers. But, although capable of producing the Me-109G, it did not do so until November 1943.

Units of the Bulgarian and Rumanian airforces could therefore play a role in defence of their countries, but in fact Luftwaffe dispositions in southern Europe were the prime consideration for would-be attackers.

Anti-aircraft unit of the Rumanian air force

Overall the Luftwaffe consisted of a number of *Luftflotten* (Air Fleets), each assigned to a particular area and sub-divided into *Fliegerkorps* for administrative purposes. Within the *Fliegerkorps* were bomber and fighter elements, of which the *Geschwader* was the largest operational unit. The *Jagdgeschwader* (JG) fighter element consisted of approximately 120 aircraft distributed between three *Gruppen*, in turn containing three *Staffeln* (each of twelve aircraft, only nine of which were simultaneously operational): these roughly equalled an RAF Group, Wing and Squadron respectively. For tactical purposes each *Staffel* operated in *Schwarm* (4-5), *Kette* (3) or *Rotte* (2) formations. Units were numbered according to their *Gruppe:* hence II/JG27 represented the second *Gruppe* of *Jagdgeschwader* 27 and the *Staffeln* were numbered consecutively within each *Geschwader*. So *Gruppe* I always had 1, 2 and 3 *Staffeln*, *Gruppe* II 4, 5 and 6. To avoid long numerical descriptions the *Gruppe* number was frequently dropped and 4/JG27 used to represent 4/II/JG27. In addition to the *Jagdgeschwader*, within the *Fliegerkorps* were such units as *Zerstoerergeschwader* (ZG) of twin-engined day fighters or *Nacht Jagdgeschwader* (NJG) of night fighters, the latter often also used in day operations. ZG and NJG units similarly carried *Staffel* and *Gruppe* numberings; and some of the latter stationed in Rumania were used against the Ploesti attackers in August 1943.

In 1943 the Luftwaffe was divided into five *Luftflotten*, of which *Luftflotte* 4 was based in Vienna. Responsible for Austria, Czechoslovakia and the Balkans (excluding Greece), it was under Colonel-General Lohr until June 1943, then General Holle. At the beginning of 1943 a special Luftwaffe Command South-East was organised for Greece under Field-Marshal Kesselring's *Luftflotte* 2, whose responsibility was Italy and the western Mediterranean. But three months later this command achieved semi-

Rumanian pilots in a JU-88

autonomous status. In the immediat
area of Ploesti units of I/JG4 (Captai
Hans Hahn) and IV/JG27 (First Lieu
tenant Burk) with Me-109s were sta
tioned at Mizil twenty miles east o
the town, plus Me-110s of IV/NJG
(Captain Lutje) at Zilistea furthe
east. Other units in Greece, Crete an
southern Italy were geographicall
in a position to attack bombers flyin
to and from Rumania, as the 194
crews discovered painfully.

In addition the Bulgarian an
Rumanian Air Forces could interven
The 6th Bulgarian Fighter Regimer
(Colonel Vasil Vulkov) was statione
near Sofia, the majority of the squac
rons equipped with Avia 534 biplane
but with some Me-109s at Karlovo
The Rumanians, however, were muc
stronger. At Perira on the outskirt
of Bucharest Major Illiescu had thre
squadrons of IAR 80 and IAR 81 air
craft and nearby were a squadron o
Rumanian-manned Ju-88s and tw
squadrons of Ju-87s. The latter migh
be used in the favourite Germa

Planes of the Rumanian JU-87 squadron prepare for takeoff

tactic of hoisting the attackers with their own petard by dropping fragmentation bombs from above, and Ju-88s were particularly effective in dealing with the slower cripples. On the Black Sea coast near Constanta more IAR 80s and Me-109s were stationed.

One striking feature about the planning stages of the Ploesti mission was the Allies' lack of accurate knowledge about enemy defences around the town. Both British and American intelligence produced reports, which were frequently based on dated material and rarely agreed on enemy strength, dispositions or capability. This was true up to the very departure of the aircraft. Moreover, most of the reports were riddled with qualifications and suspiciously round figures: at best they were vague. An RAF appreciation of 6th May indirectly admitted lack of recent information by stating that the latest knowledge of decoy towns 'believed to be' seven miles east and eight miles north-west of Ploesti was dated June 1941. Eleven days later the RAF considered that heavy and light anti-aircraft artillery, balloons and searchlights were near Ploesti in force and could be backed up by thirty Me-109Gs (none of which were then in the Balkans) and a number of Fw 190s if a serious attack occurred. Towards the end of June the British estimated 80-100 fighters, 60-100 balloons (capable of reaching 13,000 feet), 'strong' anti-aircraft guns and probably smoke in the Ploesti defences. On the last day of the month HQ RAF ME produced a more detailed summary of information. This noted that no reconnaissance photographs were available and absolute accuracy could not therefore be guaranteed: in fact, even a cursory glance reveals that some of this information had been gleaned over two years previously. The lowest estimate of the number of balloons at Ploesti was fifty, one source in February 1943 thought 'about sixty,' another a month later suggested 'well over 100'. A report of December 1941 believed each balloon, attached to a windlass by two cables, was about five metres long with ten steel rods approximately two metres in length dangling from the nose and a device, which might be a sound detector, beneath the tail. 'A source' in February 1943 thought the balloons able to fly at an altitude of 2,500 metres (8,200 feet) and one in December 1942 estimated that fifty were capable of 4,000 metres (13,000 feet). In the Ploesti/Brazi area there were about one hundred light and heavy anti-aircraft guns, the largest calibre being 88mm. Concerning Campina 'no recent information is available,' the latest being April 1941. At that time two heavy guns were located on a river bridge one mile west of the refineries, eight on the Campina-Baicoi road running south-south-east of the town and twenty-five guns distributed along the roads to Targoviste and Pitesti south-west of the town. About balloons there was no information, although a barrage was expected.

During the third week in July two further appreciations were produced by HQ RAF ME. The first estimated 80-100 mainly 88mm but 'possibly a few 105mm' heavy guns and 160-200 'usually' 20 and 37mm light anti-aircraft guns, most of them grouped in batteries under German control. About 100 searchlights and 80-100 balloons were thought to be in the Ploesti area, together with smoke apparatus (British tests showed that twenty square miles could be covered against high and low-level attack in twenty minutes). Specialised German teams were believed to be on hand to assist in fire-fighting. Approximately one hundred Me-109s, half of them normally serviceable, were 'probably' at Stresnicul and Targsorul airfields at Ploesti and manned 'mostly' by German pilots. 'Probably . . . obsolescent' Rumanian fighters were also nearby. It was estimated that thirty Me-110 night fighters were close at

A German officer gives instructions to a Rumanian light anti-aircraft gun crew

hand, but some were reported as well at Buzau (forty miles east-north-east): radar equipment was apparently concentrated on eastern and southern approaches to the town. The second of these reports stated that balloons were at varying heights and situated every 500 metres, camouflaged brick walls had been built round the oil wells with the top half conical to prevent the spread of fires, and one light anti-aircraft gun was placed at approximately 100 metre intervals round the town and oil fields. West of Ploesti stood a dummy town of wood and cardboard, as yet unfinished.

Less than a week after these reports and six days before the actual mission, RAF intelligence again admitted ignorance, by stating that information was 'urgently' required about the Ploesti refineries, aerodromes, enemy

Anti-aircraft guns were placed at approximately 100 metre intervals round the town and oilfields

fighters and balloons (their location, strength, whether they were flown twenty-four hours a day and had ordinary or lethal cables). Moreover, this plea for help asked whether there had been any recent alarms and wondered 'are the chaps in practice, i.e. Flak and ARP'.

Almost on the eve of the raid an extraordinary stroke of luck apparently occurred when, annoyed at the arrogance of German comrades-in-arms, a Rumanian pilot, Nikolai Feodor, surrendered himself and his Ju-88 at Limasol in Cyprus. When questioned he claimed that the Ploesti defences were 'very heavy' and that some 500 new gun emplacements had been built in the oil fields during Spring 1943. North of Ploesti was a dummy town capable of showing lights. The reluctant aviator helpfully suggested that escapees might make for hills north of Pitesti, where anti-German bandits roamed abroad, and revealed that special passes were needed only in certain areas like Ploesti and Bucharest. The few German troops in Rumania were guarding important installations, Feodor declared, and then indicated two airfields, Tighina and Tiraspol, not on Allied maps. Before April 1943, he claimed, there were no modern fighters in Rumania, only a few hundred old Polish aircraft – certainly not true of Luftwaffe units and probably not even of Rumanian, and therefore some indication of the value of Feodor's testimony. In fact this defector had little useful information to offer though, depressingly, he did suggest that explosive charges were attached to balloon cables.

On 28th July the final American intelligence assessment was produced based upon information available before Feodor's statements. Its admittedly sparse and dated details were due partly to a ban on aerial reconnaissance for fear that the defenders might be put on their guard. About one hundred 'medium and heavy' anti-aircraft guns, manned respectively by Rumanians and Germans were in the Ploesti area. The outer belt was believed weakest to

the south, but the inner defences to a depth of five miles round the town were 'extremely strong'. The oil fields were dotted with flak towers (not the massive concrete structures of western Europe, but simpler erections built to take small-calibre guns) and the refineries surrounded by numerous batteries. Relative weakness in heavy artillery to the south was offset by a barrage of approximately one hundred balloons – 'hundred' appeared to be something of a magic number in all Allied reports about Ploesti – believed to be anchored by cables to trucks, lowered by day but flown at night between 6,000 and 10,000 feet. A Ninth Air Force Bomber Command study pointed out that German balloons were smaller than American and British and that their cables were weaker, with no lethal device attached. A pilot confronted with a cable should attack down wind and as low as possible, for the British had found balloon cables ineffective against low-flying aircraft.

American intelligence discounted reports of dummy towns north of Ploesti but concluded that two probably existed, apparently constructed of 'paper-maché' and possibly movable at short notice. One was on the

Ploesti-Constanta railway, east of the Romana Americana refinery and seven miles from Ploesti itself; the other on the Ploesti-Bucharest railway, south of the Credituel Minier refinery at Brazi and twelve miles from Ploesti. If a smoke screen was used it would not exceed a maximum height of 360 feet. The fighter defences were known to be controlled by the Luftwaffe with aircraft at six airfields near Ploesti plus some at Bucharest. No known fighter bases were located between Benghasi and the Danube via the Adriatic, Albania and Jugoslavia. Recent information suggested that enemy radar installations were concentrated south and east of Ploesti, partly because hills to the north-west seriously reduced their efficiency.

Americans who flew the August mission found that Allied intelligence had no real idea of the extent of enemy camouflage. The roofs of tanks at the Giurgiu pumping station on the southern edge of Ploesti were painted to resemble a group of houses from the air, and Ploesti south station had white dummy roads painted across the railway lines and marshalling yards as an apparent extension of the town's boulevards, with the roofs of the station buildings made, like the Giurgiu pumping station, to look like a row of houses. Heavy guns were not confined to the outer belt of defences. Photographic evidence from the raid later revealed fifty-two 88mm guns in ten positions round the town and a number of Wurzburg RDF control centres with a group of four 88mm, two light anti-aircraft guns and a searchlight around them. Raid evidence also identified 125 light guns, many the four-barrelled 20mm Flakvierling 38, stationed close to the refineries or mounted on flak towers in groups of three, twenty-three balloons to the north and east of Ploesti (not south and east as expected) and a considerable number of smoke pots. The Official Mission Directive, Field Order 58, by Brigadier-General Ent which predicted less than a hundred anti-aircraft guns was therefore seriously astray: a figure of 250 plus machine-guns would have been more realistic, if less reassuring. Moreover the situation of Ploesti at the mouth of the Prahova Valley meant that guns mounted on ridges at the side of the

US bombers and fighters in Egypt. The decision is made to carry out the attack from a Western Desert airfield

A damaged hangar at Benina airfield,
east of Benghasi

valley were in a particularly good
position to fire on aircraft approaching
from the north-west.

It was against this background of
sparse knowledge about the current
state of enemy defences, yet mounting
pressure for action, that plans for
another attack on the Ploesti oil
refineries were discussed. With the
retirement westwards of Field-
Marshal Rommel and his Afrika
Korps there seemed little doubt that a
raid could best be flown from Western
Desert airfields, now able to cope with
the large force of heavy bombers
which the USAAF had to hand.

Within days of Halverson's attack
arrangements were made for a rapid
expansion of USAAF personnel and
facilities in the Middle East. On 28th
June 1942 Major-General Brereton arrived from India with nine B-17s of
the 9th Bombardment Squadron to
join Halverson Detachment B-24s. All
these heavy bombers henceforth came
under Brereton's command and were

soon designated the 1st Provisional
Group. B-24 reinforcements now began
to reach the Middle East in some
strength and operations were carried
out in support of the British Eighth
Army. On 12th November 1942 the
Ninth Air Force was officially established with Brereton as its Commanding-General, and a fortnight later
Ninth Air Force Bomber Command
(consisting of the 1st Provisional
and 98th Bombardment Groups) came
into being. After the land victory at
El Alamein the Ninth Air Force's two
heavy bombardment groups moved up
to Egyptian airfields at Abu Sueir,
Fayid and El Kabrit from Lydda in
Palestine where they had been stationed out of reach of enemy aircraft.
They also began to use LG 139 at
Gambut (Gambut Main) thirty miles
west of Tobruk, as a forward base for
refuelling purposes. Here the Italians
had joined two adjacent fields and so
Ninth Bomber Command had 2,000
feet of runway. By now 1st Provisional
Group had become 376 Bombardment
Group under Lieutenant-Colonel
George F McGuire, Colonel Halver-

son's replacement, and Colonel John R Kane had assumed command of the 98th.

Late in January 1943 the Egyptian bases were vacated and the remaining sections of Ninth Bomber Command moved up to Cyrenaica. Its Headquarters was located at Berka Main, with two squadrons of the 98th each at Lete and Benina, east of Benghasi, the former with an all-weather strip and deriving its name from its proximity to a stream which in olden times was believed to be a waterway to Hell (the Greek 'Lethe', river of Hades, whose waters induced forget-

Major-General Brereton (left) and General Strickland, commander of US fighters at Gambut

Brigadier-General Ent

time-fused missiles on the aircraft from above. So the Ninth Air Force did not adopt the combat box system as a policy before the second Ploesti raid: hence Eighth and Ninth Air Force Groups on that mission flew different tactical formations.

Two further B-24 Groups (the 44th and 93rd) had arrived in Britain to reinforce the Eighth Air Force. Three squadrons of the 93rd in fact gained desert experience when detached first to the Twelfth Air Force in Algeria then to the Ninth in Libya between December 1942 and February 1943. During these eighty-one days the squadrons flew twenty-two missions from desert bases, averaging nine and a half hours each but with one of eleven and a half hours. When they returned to Britain they left Lieutenant-Colonel K K Compton behind to command 376 Group of the Ninth Air Force. Compton was to lead that group over Ploesti and, in doing so, gain a Distinguished Service Cross. Meanwhile in flying from the United

fulness). 376 Group was stationed at the rough Soluch field thirty miles south of Benghasi. By mid-March the entire Ninth Bomber Command was established in the Benghasi area under Colonel (later Brigadier-General) Ent. Operations were regularly carried out over the Mediterranean against targets in Italy, but rain in Cyrenaica often caused trouble on the home airfields which, with the exception of Lete, were unmetalled. Two other all-weather strips were therefore prepared with the help of British engineers and local labour, and on 6th April 376 Group gratefully evacuated Soluch for Berka 2. On missions flown against Axis targets in southern Europe the groups proved reluctant to accept the combat box formations, which the Eighth Air Force had developed for self-protection over Germany. The need to maintain loose, rather than tight, formations was argued even more fervently when the enemy began to use air-to-air bombing by dropping

Colonel K K Compton

Kingdom 44 Group of B-24s had suffered very heavy casualties over Germany. By May 1943 only one machine, *Suzy Q*, of the 67th Squadron's original aircraft survived, and the group had such a manpower deficiency that ground crew were converted to gunners in order to man newly-arrived replacement aircraft. Nevertheless with new machines and further drafts to bring them up to strength during Spring 1943 both B-24 Groups flew successful missions, such as the combined effort against La Pallice docks on 29th May 1943 when no planes were lost. So in the United Kingdom two additional B-24 groups with operational experience, some of it in desert conditions, could be utilised by the Ploesti planners.

In January 1943 Lieutenant-Colonel C V Whitney, Assistant Air Intelligence Officer of the Ninth Air Force, submitted a plan known as Project R to Major-General Brereton for a minimum strike of forty-eight heavy bombers against six vital refineries and the main marshalling yards at Ploesti. The attack, to be carried out in daylight from bases near Aleppo in Syria, would involve violation of Turkish airspace. This particular plan was still-born due to a lack of resources in the Middle East and American commitments to support the British Eighth Army in its North African advance.

During the same month, in which the British and American leaders meeting at Casablanca discussed direction of the whole combined bomber offensive, the British Chiefs of Staff turned their attention to an all-out attack on enemy oil facilities. Sir Charles Portal maintained that this must be deferred until the fighting in North Africa had ceased 'and the whole of the Anglo-American heavy bomber resources were available for a large-scale attack on the Ploesti refineries'. Although in agreement, Sir

British and American leaders meet at Casablanca, January 1943

Colonel Jacob E Smart

mainland which would enable Ploesti to be got at, and then there are my plans for putting it across the Turks to let us fuel at their bases some time this summer'. Portal replied that the Chiefs of Staff had discussed an attack on Ploesti in January and agreed to postpone any decision until 1st April 1943. While the Allied airforces were committed to ground support in North Africa a strong attack on Ploesti was impossible and an inadequate one would only forewarn the enemy. Once fighting in North Africa was over 'we shall be in a position to bomb Ploesti either by sustained night attack or by a large-scale daylight attack, which would rely on surprise for its success'. Portal thought that bases in North Africa, Cyprus and Syria were at such extreme ranges from Rumania that even sustained attacks were 'unlikely to do effective damage,' though use of Turkish bases for refuelling would enable more bombs to be carried. However, until the Crimea or nearer

Alan Brooke nevertheless pointed out that the Axis collapse in Africa might occur suddenly and that it was 'desirable that all arrangements and plans for the air attack on the Ploesti refineries should be completed in the near future'. A fortnight later Portal told the Chiefs of Staff that 'plans for air attack on the Ploesti oil refineries by a force of twelve squadrons were in existence and were kept up-to-date in the Middle East'. The British therefore revealed no sense of urgency, possibly because they themselves had no means to carry out such a raid.

Winston Churchill personally reopened the question a month later. On the last day of February he told Portal: 'The President mentioned the matter to me casually at Casablanca, recalling that Stalin had said there would be no objection to American airplanes (sic) landing and refuelling on Russian territory. He asked why we had let it all drop'. Churchill added: 'There is also talk of the Russians reaching positions on the

Major-General Ira C Eaker

mainland bases were available, there was little point in refuelling in the USSR. In conclusion Portal stated 'We believe our best course is to deliver a single overwhelming surprise attack in daylight,' which is most interesting in view of the mission that was ultimately flown and subsequent British criticism of it. Portal felt that such an attack could be done without violation of Turkish airspace 'if essential,' in which case 'some advantage' might be derived from refuelling in the USSR. But 'to gain the maximum advantage from surprise' the attacking aircraft should fly over Turkey and the Black Sea, which was a shorter route to the target and free from enemy interference for much of the way. He emphasised that a plan for attack, always kept up todate, was available at HQ RAF ME: currently it provided for the use of eighteen squadrons – six more than Portal had mentioned to the Chiefs of Staff six weeks before. In fact this escalation of squadrons had apparently come about gradually: for on 13th February the Assistant Chief of the Air Staff, in casting doubt upon Russian administrative ability to cope with Allied refuelling, quoted ten heavy squadrons in connection with an attack on Ploesti.

During March considerable planning activity occurred on both sides of the Atlantic. In the United Kingdom views of the American Committee of Operations Analysts on the importance of oil as a target were studied by British and American authorities, and in Washington Colonel Jacob E Smart, a member of General Arnold's Army Air Forces' Advisory Council, was working on a plan for low-level attack on Ploesti from North Africa. He planned for 200 aircraft to attack nine refineries once the North African campaign ended and before the invasion of Sicily. Smart argued that about 2,400 sorties at high altitude would be required for even a partial destruction of each refinery. Such an undertaking would spread over two months, and

with each successive raid the enemy would strengthen his defences. Moreover, if this plan were adopted, the bulk of Allied heavy bombers would be exclusively committed to Ploesti for this lengthy period. Smart submitted that, although low-level bombing would be new for heavy bombers, it had been successfully used by other aircraft. General Arnold was impressed and encouraged Smart to work out a detailed plan of attack. In the middle of the month a minor security scare blew up. Part of an intercepted message between Berlin and Rome read: 'It is learned from English diplomatic circles in Ankara on 9/3 (sic) that an air attack on the Ploesti airfields has been decided upon'. Relatively unperturbed, Whitehall pointed out that the enemy must be aware of the vulnerability of Ploesti and, in any case, no firm plans had been laid, least of all concerning the 'oilfields'.

Throughout April Colonel Smart and Lieutenant-Colonel Whitney, now in Washington, both worked on separate plans for action against Ploesti. On 11th April HQ RAF ME, in reply to an Air Ministry signal, stated: 'No detailed plans for a large-scale daylight attack on Ploesti have been worked out, but up-to-date target information is available and plans could soon be prepared'. Astonishingly this message then suggested that fifty Liberators each with a 4,000-lb bomb load might attack from Gambut overflying Crete (a German-held island out of range of friendly fighter protection) and thence up the Aegean, presumably passing west of Turkey and virtually over the length of Bulgaria. Not surprisingly, considering the method proposed, success by a single attack was not expected. Furthermore '100 per cent spare refinery capacity is considered to be available' and a sustained bombing offensive might therefore be necessary to achieve success. Two days later HQ RAF ME stated that the B-17E had a radius of action of

627 statute miles with a 5,000-lb bomb load and the B-24D 700 miles with 8,000 lbs or 950 miles with 5,000 lbs. Shortly afterwards the Air Ministry told Winston Churchill that, following reconsideration, twelve to fifteen squadrons would be required for a daylight attack on Ploesti, but without use of Turkish airfields success could not be guaranteed. Only B-24s or Halifaxes could be used, as the B-17 lacked the necessary range.

Toward the end of the month the AAF Plans Division in Washington recommended an attack from Syria against the Ploesti refineries by four heavy groups with diversionary raids on Giurgiu and the Lower Danube river traffic. On 5th May Lieutenant-Colonel Whitney's plan of attack, a modification of Project R produced some four months earlier, was put forward. Whitney, like the Plans Division, favoured North Syria as a base with a minimum of one hundred aircraft bombing from high altitude against selected refinery targets. General Arnold therefore had two very different proposals before him: a low-level attack from Libya or a high-altitude one from Syria.

On 6th May a detailed feasibility study was submitted to Colonel Smart by Colonel Charles G Williamson, Air Corps Special Projects Officer, Assistant Chief of Air Staff Intelligence, who listed the refineries in order of importance on the basis of an attack by 200 bombers: Astra Romana (including Unirea Orion), Romana Americana, Concordia Vega, Unirea Sperantza (including the Standard Petrol Block), Credituel Minier (at Brazi), Steaua Romana (at Campina) and Colombia Aquila. If less than nineteen squadrons each of nine aircraft were available for the first six objectives, the attack should not be tried, and for 'complete destruction' twenty-eight squadrons of nine aircraft (252 total) were necessary to avoid further missions. A minimum-altitude attack would ensure accuracy, though Colonel Williamson suggested flying at high altitude to the target to conserve fuel. After assembly over their home bases in North Africa the aircraft should proceed to a point 150 miles west of Crete to indicate Italy as the point of attack and discourage fighter interception from the island. The force would then fly at high altitude to Slatina in Rumania, twenty-five miles north-east of Craiova, descending here to minimum altitude before making for the Initial Point at Targoviste. There the Campina aircraft would follow the railway and river north to Pucioasa and turn right to head directly for Campina, and those detailed for Brazi would turn off at Targoviste and make straight for their target. The attack could best be made from the west at sundown, when it was hoped that the setting sun would confuse the defenders and illuminate the target. Furthermore a night return to base would make interception difficult, whereas a day withdrawal 'would undoubtedly meet considerable opposition'. 250-lb American GP bombs were satisfactory, but since eight 500-lb and six 100-lb bombs plus incendiaries could be carried by a B-24 the latter load was preferable. For protection each aircraft should have three (preferably six) forward-pointing .50 machine-guns. No aircraft should exceed 300 feet and ideally be under 100 feet during the minimum-altitude phase of the attack, because over 100 feet it became progressively more easy for automatic weapons on the ground to track aircraft. To avoid ricochets lead planes in a squadron should hug the ground with others slightly stepped up behind. Williamson concluded: 'Flak positions can be best nullified by flying directly at and over them, firing forward guns, and staying as close to the ground as possible'.

General Arnold's Advisory Council in Washington believed this plan 'practicable' with modifications, but the RAF expressed scepticism unless use of the Turkish airfields could be obained. In any case the Air Ministry favoured 'a medium level' attack in view of the strength of the Ploesti defences and American success at high level in Europe. Perhaps, too, it had in mind still one more paper, this time by Group Captain Vintras, on the susceptibility of Rumanian oil to sabotage. The ghost of John Griffiths yet stalked the corridors of power. Vintras was nothing if not ambitious: sabotage of the wells might be succeeded or replaced by 'a combined operation against Constanta, followed by a land raid on Ploesti, staged as soon as possible after a Turkish declaration of war'.

Meanwhile Major-General Ira C Eaker, Commanding-General of the Eighth Air Force in Britain, had visited Washington at the end of April and told the American Joint Chiefs of Staff (JCS) that any attack upon Axis oil was 'contingent upon plans to strike the Ploesti refineries from Mediterranean bases'. Only if this succeeded would an assault upon synthetic oil be required to exploit the advantage gained. Ploesti must be the primary objective of any anti-oil campaign. A fortnight later the Combined Chiefs of Staff instructed their planning staff to treat an attack on Ploesti 'as a matter of emergency'. The RAF again argued that one low-level attack would be insufficient especially as the refineries were 'scattered and we understand that 100 per cent spare refinery capacity is available'; moreover, only Liberators could reach Ploesti from Cyrenaica. On 17th May General Arnold's Advisory Council submitted a report which considered an attack in June or early July feasible. This document was deliberately vague, advising that detailed planning be left to 'the Commanding-General of the North African Air Forces'. However, several possible bases of operation were suggested, including Aleppo and Tobruk, and a recommendation added that, if a concentration of balloons should be suspected, 'a very high altitude'

attack might be advisable.

The day after the Joint Chiefs of Staff received this report, a Combined Chiefs of Staff meeting in Washington considered the Ploesti question. Lieutenant-General Joseph T Mc-Narney (acting for General Arnold, who was indisposed) stated that, in view of the German commitment to action against the USSR, a successful attack on Ploesti would be the greatest single contribution that the Allies could make in the war at this time. The ranges to Ploesti from Tobruk, Aleppo, Alexandria, Cyprus and Tripoli respectively were 875, 835, 963, 755 and 1,080 miles, and from these bases B-24Ds with 6,000 lbs of bombs, B-24Cs with 3,000 lbs and possibly B-17Fs could attack. McNarney believed that 155 aircraft would be needed; only a few enemy fighters were in the Ploesti area 'and the main defence [is] provided by a balloon barrage, mainly to the south'. Operating from Tobruk, the aircraft could pass out of radar range of Crete and an attack at dusk would enable a return to base in darkness. The attack, possibly led by Major-General Doolittle, would probably be low level: 'losses might be heavy, but would be more than offset by results'. The CCS agreed that Arnold should forward these suggestions to General Dwight D Eisenhower, Commander-in-Chief North African Theatre, for his comments.

Plans now crystallised rapidly. Two days later the attack on Ploesti was allocated the codename 'STATES-MAN' and next day the Allied Trident Conference agreed that two B-24 groups from the United Kingdom (the 93rd and 44th) should be assigned to the project for about four weeks and a third group (the 389th), destined for the Eighth Air Force in England, should be added to the mission force straight from its initial training in the USA. Sir Charles Portal pointed out that execution of the mission now would divert aircraft from preparations for 'HUSKY' (the invasion

Trident Conference; from left to right,
General Sir Alan Brooke, Air Marshal
Sir Charles Portal, and Field-Marshal
Sir John Dill

of Sicily) and that a partially successful raid would make future
operations extremely difficult. The
American Army Chief of Staff,
General Marshall, argued that 'even
if fairly successful' a heavy blow
would be dealt to the enemy; and on

24th May Colonel Smart arrived in
North Africa to explain the project to
General Eisenhower. In consequence
Eisenhower signalled next day: 'The
prize is a great one. Both Tedder
[Air Commander-in-Chief Mediter-
ranean] and I are anxious to do the
job,' but expressed some concern at
the loss of bomber sorties for HUSKY
preparations. The mission had therefore become a matter of fact rather
than speculation. On the same day

that Eisenhower signalled his qualified support, the codename was changed to 'SOAPSUDS' and 23rd June set as a tentative mission date for planning purposes. During the period 18th–25th May, the decision to attack Ploesti again had thus effectively been taken after months of doubt, although many planning hurdles had yet to be cleared.

Towards the end of May, General Marshall formally warned Major-General Eaker that his two B-24 groups would be involved in 'STATES-MAN' (as it was then known). But the RAF still considered an attack on Ploesti unwise until use of Turkish airfields was assured, and on 2nd June the Air Ministry noted: '. . . in view of poor American equipment and lack of basic training in map reading, navigation may be their major difficulty'. It suggested that three RAF Lancasters might lead the attack. Air Officer Commanding-in-Chief RAF Bomber Command, Air Chief Marshal Sir Arthur Harris, agreed with this idea and proposed to put it to Eaker,

The Air Ministry put forward the suggestion that RAF Lancasters might lead the attack

Air Chief Marshal Sir Arthur 'Bomber' Harris

although HQ RAF ME felt (correctly) that Americans would scarcely welcome the implications of his suggestion.

Meanwhile Eisenhower finally put aside doubts and agreed that SOAPSUDS was 'an important and desirable operation,' which should be carried out by five heavy bombardment groups at the end of the July, not June. The Combined Chiefs of Staff took note of British and American fears about HUSKY and laid down that its success should not be prejudiced by SOAPSUDS. Field-Marshal Dill signalled that Washington had agreed that the two Eighth Air Force groups and the 389th should go to the Middle East; on 15th June Eaker told Marshall that eighty aircraft of the

93rd and 44th Groups were ready to go. A week earlier Marshall had informed the Americans Joint Chiefs of Staff of Winston Churchill's fear that other German-controlled refineries might make good oil deficiencies in Rumania and that, in any case, the USSR would not feel benefit from any attack for from one to three months. On the same day, however, the Combined Chiefs of Staff ordered Eisenhower to carry out SOAPSUDS 'at the earliest practicable date provided that it does not on any account prejudice HUSKY or risk failure through inadequate time for preparation'.

Ten days later Colonel Smart revealed his latest (though not final) plan to a conference at HQ RAF ME in Cairo. He proposed a co-ordinated

attack of not less than 150 aircraft. B-24s and a force of B-17s would fly from Benghasi to Corfu in the Adriatic, where the B-17s would turn west to attack Italy, while the B-24s went on to bomb seven selected refineries in Ploesti at dusk from low level. For this purpose, 1,000-lb HE, clusters of incendiaries and 65-lb oil-filled bombs would be used. On 1st July the code-name was again changed, for the last time, to 'TIDALWAVE'. Four days later Brereton complained that some 44 Group aircraft were still in the United Kingdom, and these were subsequently despatched. At one stage more aircraft than full crews were in Cyrenaica, but fresh arrivals came direct from the USA to repair this deficiency. Not all authorities were

General Eaker's Eighth Airforce 'Flying Fortresses' take off for a raid on Germany

yet convinced that the mission was worthwhile. On 10th July the Air Officer Commanding-in-Chief Middle East, Air Chief Marshal Sir Sholto Douglas, having studied details of TIDALWAVE, signalled Headquarters Mediterranean Air Command: 'I am firmly of the opinion that a sufficient degree of destruction is most unlikely – repeat unlikely – to be achieved by a single low-level attack'. He estimated that at least five subsequent high-altitude raids would be necessary. Ten days later, and only twelve before the actual mission, its abandonment was urged by Major-General Eaker who wanted all Eighth Air Force planes concentrated in the United Kingdom for action against Germany. Eisenhower urged General Marshall not to call off the attack, but did sound a note of caution: 'Both Tedder and Spaatz [Commanding-General of the Twelfth Air Force in Algeria] are of the conviction that we must carry out more than one attack in the TIDALWAVE operation' and that, if 'reasonable success' could be achieved in the first, subsequent raids must aim for a total of 60–70 per cent destruction. Both Marshall and Arnold in Washington agreed that the mission should proceed. But shortly afterwards Major-General Brereton noted that one low-level attack would not suffice, estimating that eight further high-altitude attacks with an average strength of 136 bombers would be required.

Whilst argument continued between high-ranking officers and politicians, several specific attempts were made to boost the mission's chance of success. When originally informed of STATESMAN, Eaker was told to equip all Eighth Air Force planes involved with low-level bomb sights. Thus on arrival in North Africa they all had the N7 sight fitted: this was a modified gun sight and replaced the Norden equipment which had been developed for high-altitude bombing. At the end of May the Air Ministry in London agreed to fix British DR compasses and air-speed indicators to as many STATESMAN aircraft as possible, though in the event only eighteen did receive these items of equipment. To help neutralise flak and small-arms positions, additional guns were fitted in the noses of B-24s in the leading flights of each target force (most carried twin .50 machine-guns) and the dorsal (top) turrets were modified to permit forward-firing; more armour was also added to the flight deck. Crew members who would be non-operational during the actual bombing run (like the radio operator and flight engineer) were

issued with sub-machine-guns for use through the waist windows. Extra fuel tanks were fitted to the wings as well as in the bomb-bay and arrangements made for 150 new engines to replace those prematurely aged by the desert sand, which sometimes reduced the life of a Pratt and Whitney engine from 300 hours to a mere 60. Possibly as many as 300 new engines arrived at Benghasi in the liner *Mauretania* two days before the Ploesti attack.

Very valuable training aids were also developed in the form of models of the Ploesti area and the individual refineries, built from details available to the Allies from pre-war records and the personal observations of former oil refinery employees. Five models were constructed of Ploesti, Brazi and Campina (each of the scale 1/50,000), and the general areas of Floresti-Ploesti (1/100,000) and Campina (1/500,000). These models included all natural features, ground undulations, trees etc. and were extremely well produced. Fifteen large-scale photographs of these models were then taken and perspective sketches made of the individual targets. Utilmately each crew had sketches, maps and photographs to cover the advance to its Aiming Point and the precise lay-out of its individual target. In addition copies of eleven small-scale maps of the general area (1/1,000,000 or 1/500,000) were printed in large quantities.

These models were built under strict security precautions at RAF Medmenham in Buckinghamshire, and here too they were used to make a special 16mm film of forty minutes duration. This film, designed to give crews an idea of actually attacking the target, was accompanied by an explanatory commentary. It contained general information for all crew members plus special sections for pilots, navigators and bombardiers, with the aim of getting uniformity of briefing for all those involved in the mission. Silent 8mm films were also produced to show the approach to each individual target, based upon further models of the refineries which had been constructed after the original five. The very existence of this elaborate collection of films, models and maps emphasised the depth of planning for this one operation.

On 17th June Colonel Smart reported to General Eisenhower: 'Models are considered very good. Target folders being prepared here [in the United Kingdom]. Briefing movie being filmed from models, maps, photographs and perspective drawings, and should be completed by 25th June'. The man primarily responsible for the films and models was Wing Commander A P H Forbes, whose efforts did not immediately earn a Whitehall accolade. The Air Ministry noted on 8th July that Forbes 'has done remarkably well in the short time and with the material available . . . [but the 16mm] film has a considerable number of defects such as scale of maps, orientation of display, lack of definition of important detail and perspective during low-level approach'. Air Chief Marshal Sir Arthur Tedder agreed that the film was 'disappointing' because it was impossible to simulate a really low approach and Lieutenant-Colonel W L Forster at Headquarters Ninth Bomber Command was equally unimpressed. The film commentary, inevitably based on intelligence information available at the end of June, in the light of actual raid experiences could certainly be faulted: 'The fighter defences at Ploesti are not strong and the majority of the fighters will be flown by Rumanian pilots who are thoroughly bored with the war' was one example of sublime nonsense. But much harsh pre-raid criticism of Forbes' efforts by RAF officers was not justified. After the mission pilots and navigators enthused about the accuracy of both the silent and talking films.

To assist navigators a map about 23 inches square was so pasted together and folded that separate maps were not required, and a printed strip 6½ inches wide and 33 long was fastened with paper clips along its left-hand edge. This had eleven sketches or photographs of important check points along the route from Corfu to the Danube and resembled an extended version of those concertina postcards which offer a number of views of their subject. In addition to maps, perspective drawings of targets were produced for each crew designed to show its own individual Aiming Point. Elaborate means to assist escapees from shot-down crews were developed too: apart from small compasses and a silk map, each man would be issued with an escape purse containing six American dollars, 3,000 Greek drachmas and 1,500 Italian lire. There was also discussion of the intricate details of the types and position of cameras to be carried in the aircraft to record details of the raid, and about follow-up reconnaissance by RAF Mosquitoes.

By 3rd July the bulk of the three reinforcement groups had arrived to join Ninth Air Force Bomber Command. 93 Group left the United Kingdom on the evening of 25th June, the 44th two days later and the newest group from the USA, the 389th, on 2nd July: travelling from Portreath in Cornwall via Oran in Algeria, they reached Benghasi after a one day flight. However, as replacement crews were slow to reach the United Kingdom, the last of the 123 B-24s did not leave Portreath until 9th July: one aircraft had already crashed flying into that base and another was forced down with engine trouble in neutral Portugal en route to Benghasi So 122 aircraft actually arrived. Already the two Eighth Air Force Groups had flown several low-level practice missions over East Anglia at tree-top height in tight formation. On 11th June the 389th landed at Hethel, Norfolk, and flew similar training missions. Although it had recently practised low-level flying in the

USA, two B-24s collided, killing eighteen. The two survivors were to go to Ploesti. Once in North Africa the 389th received its baptism of fire over Crete, and all five groups destined to fly to Ploesti carried out 1,183 sorties against seventeen Italian and other South European targets during the first three weeks of July. Apart from the numerical loss of aircraft and crews allocated to TIDALWAVE, another specific danger emerged during these missions: on 19th July one of the crews shot down included two officers already briefed for the Ploesti raid.

The newly-arrived groups were all within twenty miles of Benghasi: the 93rd occupied Site 7 (Terria) eighteen miles south of the town and west of the main north-south highway, the 44th Benina airfield twelve miles east of Benghasi and north of the Benghasi-Barse road and the 389th a base near Cast, seven miles south of Benghasi, three miles south of Berka 2 and west of the main north-south highway. Whilst the groups settled into their dusty surroundings, savoured the delights of bully beef and became accustomed to action in the Mediter-

ranean theatre, planners were developing the final details of the operation. In the last week of June, Major-General Brereton established a Planning Committee of officers to examine the project, including the relative worth of high and low-level attacks. On the day after Colonel Smart reached Benghasi, 25th June, eight officers (including Brigadier-General Ent and Colonel Edward J Timberlake, former 93rd Group Commander and now heading 201st Provisional Combat Wing of the Eighth Air Force) attended its inaugural session. The committee estimated that one low-level attack would cost sixteen aircraft per group, against twelve for a total of ten high-altitude missions. But, at this stage, it was felt that insufficient data existed to make a firm recommendation and urged both meteorological and intelligence officers to secure further information. Nevertheless, Colonel Timberlake was instructed to prepare a training programme and Colonel Snow a plan of operations based upon a low-level attack. Already it had been decided firmly to attack from Benghasi, not Aleppo. Although the

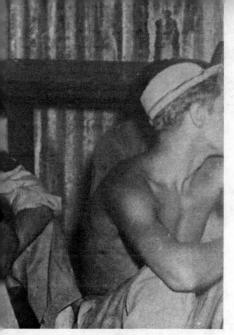

latter was closer to the target, from there Turkish neutrality would perforce be violated and the logistic problems of dealing with five groups in Syria were immense. Need for surprise, however, was the decisive factor. 200 aircraft from Aleppo could have only one objective, whereas planes from Benghasi might be attacking a variety of South European targets.

Brigadier-General Ent asked eight civilian specialists of the Ninth Bomber Command's Operations Analysis Section to look more closely into the matter. Based upon their findings he presented his views to Brereton on 30th June. If a high-altitude approach were adopted, Ent thought that 'definitely' 50 per cent of the target would be destroyed in four missions; and there was a better than evens chance that greater damage would be attained in fewer missions. If the necessary replacement engines arrived and an 80 per cent maintenance efficiency could be achieved, four missions would be possible in nine days for a total loss of twenty-two aircraft. In a high-altitude attack, furthermore, crew morale would be

better and need for a lengthy training programme would be removed. Ent accepted that low-level attack offered a better chance of complete destruction, but said: '[I] cannot help feel that 50 per cent destruction is the best thing that can be hoped for'. A fortnight's special training would be required and, he estimated, one low-level attack would cost seventy-five aircraft. He therefore recommended: 'To attack at High Level until the target is destroyed or satisfactorily neutralised'.

Brereton also received an intelligence assessment on the effect of high and low-level attack on Ploesti, and at a conference in Cairo on 1st July he summarised the position. The high-altitude method would need two direct hits by 500-lb bombs on nine aiming points (one in each refinery). To achieve this 1,761 sorties over the target were necessary and, allowing a 0–5 per cent loss rate, this would entail twenty missions of 120 aircraft each over three months, probably with a loss of 170 aircraft. A low-level attack needed to hit twenty-seven aiming points with a total of 141 1,000-lb bombs (based upon 20 per cent accuracy). For this 106 aircraft were required over the target. Taking into account losses, 200 aircraft must be used in such a mission, which had a better than evens chance of complete success for the loss of 71 aircraft. There was, however, the possibility that a low-level attack might achieve little and incur such casualties that insufficient aircraft would remain to carry out any follow-up. Fully realising that a low-level attack might involve 'possible expenditure of the entire force', because the target was vital Brereton favoured this method, followed by as many missions (at high or low level) as necessary. This decision may have been influenced by reports of heavy anti-aircraft guns

near Ploesti, which would particularly affect high-altitude aircraft. The Air Officer Commanding-in-Chief RAF Middle East, Air Chief Marshal Douglas, agreed that a low-level attack followed by high-altitude raids should be carried out, but both he and Brereton emphasised that one low-level raid would not be enough. This opinion was reiterated a week later by HQ RAF ME to the Air Ministry in London.

Meanwhile Colonel Smart had drawn up his final mission plan. He aimed to put the nine major Ploesti refineries out of action for at least four months by attacking seventeen distillation and nine cracking units: a sufficient bomb-load for this could be carried by 75 aircraft, but to allow for losses, errors and abortives, a minimum of 150 aircraft must be allocated. If missions in support of HUSKY were stopped at least a week before the raid, 80 per cent serviceability could be expected and therefore, to ensure 150, 188 aircraft should be detailed for the five groups on the day of the mission.

Brereton's planning staff at Benghasi was now being assisted by a number of experts like Group Captain D G Lewis of the RAF, who joined Colonels Smart, Stroh and Timberlake in the small planning group at Benghasi specifically responsible for TIDALWAVE. Everything connected with the mission was put under guard in a portable green shack, set up in the command compound at Berka Main: all but a few were barred from its secrets. Here the relative merits of distillation plants, cracking units and boiler houses (the latter important not only in the refinery process, but because steam was an effective firefighting weapon), were discussed. Ultimately forty targets were selected and grouped together into seven big targets, five of which were at Ploesti,

Preparing a B-24 at 376th Group's base, Berka 2

with one each at Campina and Brazi.

After considerable thought about the technical merits of available bombs and fuses, it was decided to use 1,000-lb and 500-lb bombs, the former with tail fuses timed to explode one to six hours after being dropped, the latter with as little as 45-second fuses. To ensure efficient action M-106 and M-124 fuses were specially brought from the USA. In addition, because of fire risk in the targets, all aircraft were to carry British 4-lb or American 100-lb incendiaries. Ten days before the mission one aircraft from each group was loaded with the ammunition, bombs and petrol which would be carried to Ploesti and given a flight plan similar to that envisaged for TIDALWAVE. The average flight time then proved to be 11 hrs.12mins. and the average fuel consumption 2,280 gallons at just over 202 gallons an hour.

Once details of the seven targets had been settled and operations in support of HUSKY had been suspended, the five groups commenced a rigorous training programme. South of Benghasi on the edge of an escarpment stood a ruined castle, from which a straight desert road went west to Soluch some twenty miles away. The planners used this to represent the railway line which ran from the chosen Initial Point (Floresti) to Ploesti. They worked out a dummy target area, based upon knowledge of locations in Rumania, the turning capacity of the B-24 of one degree per second and a speed of 180mph. Under the direction of Wing Commander J S Streater and Lieutenant-Colonel S L Brown, 835th Engineers, steel girders were erected to represent the refinery targets and, for ease of identification from the air, were topped with mattresses. Unfortunately local nomads nefariously purloined these latter prizes and the strips of rag which replaced them. Ultimately they could find no use for the perforated five gallon oil drums which were fixed instead on the girders. Their activities, nevertheless, had already belied official claims of security: 'The area of the dummy target was carefully guarded, only military personnel being allowed to enter'.

During the training period, which started on 20th July under Colonel Timberlake's direction, flying commenced at 500 feet, but was progressively lowered; element and flight leaders were taught one lead position and alternative flight leaders flew as co-pilots. Crews were required to drop their bombs at a maximum height of 300 feet with a maximum circular error of 100 feet: they must navigate to the target at minimum height and make no more than a five degree corrective turn between Initial Point and target. Flights of six aircraft were trained to take off within ten minutes, change from route into attacking formations during the turn from the Initial Point to the axis of attack, bomb from 300 feet and resume minimum-altitude formation afterwards. The programme allowed for bombing by individual aircraft, elements of three and waves of six and twelve. Between 22nd and 29th July particularly intensive training took place, each aircraft attacking its own section of the target with dummy bombs and the total time of all units over the target being reduced to one minute. Twelve practice missions were flown against the desert mock-up to good effect: one airman later said, 'when we finally did get over the real Ploesti, our movements were almost automatic'. Two full-scale mock missions were flown on 28th and 29th July, in the last of which live 100-lb bombs with delayed-action fuses were used and the target theoretically destroyed in two minutes. Watching from a circling B-24 Brereton reported: 'They reached the target on split-second schedule and bombed with deadly accuracy'.

Towards the end of this training, confidence rose as accuracy in navigation and bombing increased and crews became more familiar with their target. Lieutenant-Colonel W L Forster, a British adviser who proved no light critic, noted that the practice missions 'achieved a very remarkable degree of proficiency without accident' – which conveniently ignored the demise of one camel and disintegration of a number of native tents. Forster further remarked: 'The men began to feel much less afraid of the unknown and during the last five days or so, morale improved to the point where the majority of the men were actually eager to go and perform the task'. Colonel Leon W Johnson, who would win a Congressional Medal of Honour over Ploesti, said: 'There was no problem of accuracy . . . we could hit a target not much bigger than the door of a house . . . so we knew that if we could get to the target we could hit [it]'.

Crew members were told of the plans on different occasions. On 20th July group commanders, flight leaders and deputy flight leaders attended a briefing which included the exhortation: 'The piecemeal destruction of the Rumanian refineries will not have the desired effect. Destruction must be complete and final . . . You must do the job virtually in one day'. They were then addressed by Brigadier-General Ent on the defences of Ploesti, and Major G K Geerlings, Intelligence Officer of the Eighth Air Force, described details of the mission using the 16mm film and Medmenham models. Thereafter these officers were allowed access to one large room stocked with general information and the separate rooms with special details for each target force. Not until four days later were the remaining officers briefed and on 29th July enlisted men were officially told their fate.

At first crews were far from enthusiastic. Lieutenant-Colonel Forster, who attended the group commanders' briefing and stayed at Benghasi till after the mission, reported: 'The atmosphere was almost as bad as it could possibly be and morale was at its lowest: they had never done low-level work before, they had never done such a long trip before: they understood that it was one of the best defended targets in Europe . . . they were terribly afraid of the reputed balloon barrage, they expected that the installations would blow up beneath them as soon as the bombs landed'. Gradually confidence grew as American and British officers dealt with questions and explained specific points about low-level attacks, balloon barrages etc. Forster thought that these officers 'did a tremendous amount of good work', which together with the desert practice missions helped enormously to raise morale.

On Saturday 31st July Major-General Brereton, Air Chief Marshal Tedder and Brigadier-General Ent made a final tour of the camps. To one group Tedder said: 'I'm proud to be here with you just before the job. I want to wish you the best of luck in it. It's a hard, dangerous mission. It will take all your famous American courage and resourcefulness'. To every group Brereton emphasised that this mission could accomplish in one day what ground forces might need a year to do.

In the second week of July Ninth Air Force meteorologists reported that, within the period 15th July – 10th August, the 1st to the 4th of August would be the best time for attack. This conclusion was assisted by experts who had broken the cypher used by enemy meteorologists. The cypher was changed on the first of the month, hence in case of difficulty with the new one, an attack at the end of July or very early in August would be preferable. On 22nd July Brereton set the date for Saturday 31st July. Six days later this was put back to 1st August, partly because on a Sunday the enemy might be less alert and the refineries contain fewer Rumanian civilians. As the sun set over the Benghasi airfields on 31st July crews showed that mixture

Colonel Leon W Johnson

of fear, elation and resignation which inevitably precedes a dangerous mission. Brereton had already signalled General Arnold in Washington: 'I am thoroughly pleased with the attitude of all commanders . . . and the planning has been excellent . . . I think every possible contingency has been considered, and feel confident'.

Nevertheless that night few slept at Berka Main or the surrounding camps: fitful dozing was achieved at best. On the morrow great deeds would be done, heroes emerge and men die; to those who, unable to rest, sought solitude under the night sky or chatted aimlessly to defeat the waiting hours, the enormity of the task ahead was plain. The possibility of a trouble-free 'milk run' was extremely remote. Yet, such is human nature that many were buoyed up by the hope that their particular machine would emerge from the turmoil of battle unscathed. Very few were to have this hope fulfilled.

Tidalwave
1st August 1943

Before dawn at approximately 0400 (all raid times are Eastern European, two hours ahead of Greenwich Mean Time, as used in Rumania: the Benghasi bases following Egyptian Summer Time were three hours ahead, so local time was 0500) on Sunday 1st August jeeps began dashing backwards and forwards across the five mission airfields: Lete (98 Group), Berka 2 (376), Berka 4 (389), Benina Main (44) and Terria or Site 7 (93). Shortly after blaring horns and blazing lights had stirred the bases into ant-like activity, men started to trudge through dust towards the mess halls, chatting, joking or silent under the strain of impending action. Take-off was still some time away. Breakfast, collection of flying kit, parachutes and escape equipment, last-minute briefings and a ride out to the aircraft lay head. For TIDALWAVE crews this process, often up to three hours in length, would be shortened; for normally the target destination was not revealed until this pre-raid period. But they could not escape the tedious wait beside their aircraft, which, following initial equipment checks on arrival, they were forced to endure before the order to climb aboard and fuse bombs. Even then there remained the wait for the Very-pistol signal to join the crocodile of machines crawling in a pre-determined file towards the head of the runway for take-off. Today all this would take a mere two hours, of which the last forty-five minutes, when the men sat in their flying positions in the aircraft waiting for the red flare, would be the worst.

When crews left their tents, many for the last time, the occasional roar of engines could be heard as mechanics made final adjustments to machines at the dispersal points. Several ground crews had worked throughout the night, their well-intentioned efforts further disturbing the restless camps.

Aircrew member fastens on his flak suit before a raid on Ploesti, August 1st 1943

Ahead of the air crews lay a minimum twelve to thirteen hours flight, involving a 2,700-mile round trip, half of it directly over enemy-held territory. This mission would take the B-24s close to their extreme operational range of 3,500 miles, which allowed comparatively little margin for error, damage or tactical manoeuvres. The sceptical pointed out that theoretical radii of operation were calculated on the basis of peaceful flights at 160mph by planes which had not been patched up, subjected to enemy action or abused by desert sand. Many mission members were not entirely quietened by confident assurances that extra fuel tanks would be adequate to cope with the lengthy flight plan and the weight of additional fuselage-armour, ammunition and a 5,000-lb bomb load. The TIDALWAVE route was clearly based upon Colonel Smart's original concepts without the plan for a diversionary B-17 attack over Italy, not the RAF's route over Crete nor Lieutenant-Colonel Whitney's from Aleppo. Without deviation for tactical purposes or to avoid natural obstacles, the route measured 1,060 miles from Benghasi to Ploesti and 1,015 miles for the return leg. The five groups were to take off individually and assemble over their own airfields, then proceed to the mission assembly line Benghasi-Driana-Tocra on the southern Mediterranean coast, where route formation would be picked up at 0730. From the North African shore the aircraft would assume a north-north-westerly course for Corfu 500 miles away, passing 200 miles west of Crete and 100 miles west of Morea, hopefully out of enemy fighter and radar range. The force would penetrate the Ionian Sea between Italy and Greece to a point (38°20′ N, 20°08′E seventy-five miles south of Corfu. Although no known radar installations existed on Corfu, danger of visual sightings and reports made it necessary to climb to 10,000 feet to cross the island – a plan to pass to the

west also was abandoned for fear of detection and interception from the heel of Italy. Once clear of Corfu the aircraft would reach the area of the small island of Erikousa in the Straits of Otranto and turn onto a north-easterly course for a point (43° 50′N, 23° 43′E) near the Bulgarian town of Lom on the Danube 420 miles away. The strips attached to the navigators' maps would be particularly useful during this part of the route, much of which was over very hilly country.

Having crossed the Albanian coast, the force almost immediately would need to negotiate mountains up to 8,000 feet. The planned route took it a mere twenty miles east of Vlone (Valona) and eighty miles east of Tirane (Tirana) to cross the border with Jugoslavia just north of Lake Ohridska. Thereafter the mountains of Macedonian Jugoslavia rose to 8,500 feet and were relieved only by the massive River Morava, which flowed into the Danube near Belgrade and had several tributaries in Jugo-

slavia. Over Jugoslavia the aircraft would pass just west of Skopje and almost directly above Vranje to Pirot on the River Nisava, which entered the Morava at Nis, forty miles to the north-west. During this part of their journey the aircraft would fly sixty miles west of Sofia. From Pirot sixty miles south-south-west of Lom, the force was to descend, as it traversed forty miles of the north-western tip of Bulgaria, to cross the Danube at 3–5,000 feet. This lower height was necessary to take the aircraft below the level of surrounding hills, possibly surmounted by radar sites.

Once across the Danube the mission force would adopt an east-north-easterly course flying east of Craiova and west of Slatina towards the Rumanian road centre of Pitesti on the River Arges 110 miles away, which was the First Initial Point. Here one group (389) would fly towards Campina forty-eight miles north-east, the other four make for their Second Initial Point at Floresti, thirteen

miles north-west of Ploesti, to deliver their attacks.

The route formation to be adopted at the assembly line Benghasi-Driana-Tocra was based on the distribution of forces to attack TIDALWAVE targets in Rumania. The seven refinery targets had been assigned code names: WHITE 1 (Romana Americana), WHITE 2 (Concordia Vega), WHITE 3 (Standard Petrol Block and Unirea Sperantza), WHITE 4 (Astra Romana and Unirea Orion) and WHITE 5 (Colombia Aquila), all at Ploesti; BLUE (Credituel Minier, Brazi) and RED (Steaua Romana, Campina). Twenty-four aircraft from 376 Group would attack six key installations at WHITE 1 in four waves of six with Colonel Keith K Compton as target force commander. Originally, Compton's aircraft was detailed to lead this group and therefore the whole mission force, but at the last minute Lieutenant Brian W Flavelle took the lead position. Behind the 376th flew 93 Group with Lieutenant-Colonel

Above: B-24s on the Tidalwave route.
Below: Lieutenant-Colonel Addison E Baker

Above: A low-flying B-24 over target White 4, Astra Romana. *Right:* The camouflaged Colombia Aquila refinery. *Below:* Target Blue, Credituel Minier, after a hit by Lieutenant-Colonel Posey's B-24s

Addison E Baker as commander of Target Forces WHITE 2 and 3. Twenty-one of the 93rd's aircraft in three waves of six and one of three led by Major George S Brown were to attack six installations in WHITE 2, and in the route formation were followed by twelve other 93rd aircraft destined for three installations in WHITE 3 in four waves of three led by Major Ramsey D Potts. Behind the 93rd came Colonel John R Kane's 98 Group, whose forty aircraft, led by Lieutenant John S Young (who in the event flew as Kane's co-pilot) would attack WHITE 4's ten key installations in four waves of ten; and to their rear flew 44 Group. Fifteen of its aircraft in five waves of three with Colonel Leon W Johnson as target force commander and Major William H Brandon leading (Johnson acted as his co-pilot) were to attack six installations in WHITE 5 and another eighteen under Lieutenant-Colonel James T Posey's command and led by Captain John H Diehl (with Posey as co-pilot) would

attack three installations in Target
BLUE in three waves of six. The 389th,
occupying last place in the mission
force under Colonel Jack W Wood's
command and led by Captain Kenneth
M Caldwell, aimed to fly its twenty-
four aircraft in eight waves of three
against Target RED. Although the
target forces were to fly in this order,
the refineries were listed in a different
order of importance: Astra Romana
(including Unirea Orion), Concordia
Vega, Romana Americana, Steaua
Romana, Unirea Sperantza (including
Standard Petrol Block), Credituel
Minier and Colombia Aquila. In addition to the 154 planned for above,
twenty-three spare aircraft successfully took off and were allocated as
follows to compensate for aborts or
losses before the target: WHITE 1 (4),
WHITE 2 (4), WHITE 4 (6), WHITE 5
(2), BLUE (2), RED (5), with WHITE 3
receiving no spares.

The formations flown within groups
during the approach to the Second
Initial Points were varied, allowing
maximum freedom of action with a
minimum of horizontal dispersion,
and took into account normal group
tactics. The 376th and two leading
squadrons of the 93rd were to fly a
single-space, stagger formation, the
other two squadrons of the 93rd and
three of the 98th a 'V' formation; the
trailing 98th squadron and all four of
the 44th would adopt an echelon with
the 389th in the rear using a 'V' formation. Optimistically the whole mission
force would adopt a route speed of
190–210mph, though in practice it
averaged about 160mph.

At Pitesti, the First Initial Point,
all five groups would descend to minimum altitude (500 feet), further
dropping to bombing level (100—300
feet) at the Second Initial Point -
north of Campina and Floresti respectively. The four groups en route

**Oil installations ablaze at Steaua
Romana, Colonel Jack Wood's 389th
Group's Target Red**

to Floresti would pass over wooded hills and ravines unlikely to conceal anti-aircraft guns and also Targoviste, an old town with several churches and ruins of the ancient palace of the Princes of Wallachia. Like Floresti it stood at the head of a valley with a railway running southeast along it. This similarity was to lead to a tragic mis-identification during the TIDALWAVE mission; for this railway line ran to Bucharest, not Ploesti.

Over Floresti (represented in training by the ruined castle on the desert escarpment) the main force would assume the attack formation of six target forces. Within each target force individual elements were assigned specific places so that aircraft could pinpoint their own Aiming Points: all of this had been practised meticulously over Cyrenaica during the last twelve days. Once the target forces had assembled during the turn into line abreast, the formation would read from left to right Target Forces WHITE 1-5, with respective spacings of 6,250, 7,000, 2,000 and 940 feet and all left of the Floresti-Ploesti railway, for which the road from the castle to Soluch had doubled in North Africa: the spread of these five target forces would be approximately 4.3 miles. Right of the railway line would fly Target Force BLUE, proceeding individually to Brazi. From their Second Initial Points, once in attacking formation, the Target WHITE Forces would fly a heading of 127 degrees, those attacking Targets BLUE and RED 132 and 150 degrees respectively. Each target force was to fly under a single leader until individual targets were sighted, then sub-leaders would assume control: all attacking aircraft were to adopt close wing-tip to wing-tip formations. To avoid damage from bomb explosions to rear aircraft attacking waves in each target force would be stepped up from front to rear.

Once bombing had been completed the Target WHITE forces would continue on their attack course at the lowest level possible allowed by chimneys and other obstructions for varying periods of time after crossing the railway which ran west to east round the south of Ploesti: Target Forces WHITE 1, 2 and 3 for two minutes fifteen seconds, WHITE 4 two minutes and WHITE 5 one minute forty-five seconds. After this all were to turn right to a heading of 233 degrees and proceed at an altitude of 3–5,000 feet to Lake Balta Potelel on the Rumanian side of the Danube some 120 miles south-west of Ploesti and thirty miles north-west of Pleven (Plevna), a place of considerable significance in Rumanian and European history. Both Target Forces BLUE and RED were also to turn right as soon as possible after hitting their objectives onto respective courses of 233 and 220 degrees, hug the ground then climb when safe to 3–5,000 feet and head for the general rally point at Lake Balta Potelel. Here the seven target forces would resume the route formation adopted on the outward journey and climb to 10,000 feet. The mission force would not follow an identical outward and homeward route, however. On the way back, from the rally point, course would be set for the southern tip of Corfu, initially by striking south-west from Lake Balta Potelel towards Berkovista seventy miles away. This route would take the aircraft forty miles east of Pirot and only twenty west of Sofia to cross the Jugoslavian border close to Mount Kom – implying small regard for the abilities of the Bulgarian Air Force. Flying forty miles east of Skopje and ten east of Bitola, the returning B-24s would not fly over Albania, but roughly follow its border with Greece on the Greek side, taking them just west of Ioannina to Cape Asprokavos, the southern tip of Corfu. From here route formation would no longer be compulsory and aircraft could set an individual course at the most economical altitude for home bases in Africa some 500 miles away,

The bomb-load actually carried by he whole mission force was 623,000 bs. Target Force WHITE 1 took wenty-four 1,000-lb bombs (with 1-6-iour delay tail fuse), thirty-six 500-lb 1-6-hour fuse) and seventy-two 500-lb 45-second fuse) making a total of 132, gainst an estimated eighty-four eeded to destroy this target. In addiion each aircraft carried two boxes f British incendiaries. Those of 'arget Force WHITE 2 also theoreticlly required eighty-four bombs, but ad forty-eight 1,000-lb (1-hour fuse) nd fifty-four 500-lb (45-second fuse) or a total of 102 plus forty-two boxes f British incendiaries; Target Force VHITE 3 required forty-eight bombs nd took twenty-four 1,000-lb (1-hour use) and thirty-six 500-lb (45-second use) for a total of 60 plus twenty-four oxes of British incendiaries. Target 'orce WHITE 4 carried the heaviest oad against one target: needing 180 ombs, the number was made up of 20 1,000-lb (1-hour fuse) and sixty 00 lb (45-second fuse) bombs with ighty boxes of British incendiaries; nd Target Force WHITE 5 carried ight less than its estimated eighty ombs with thirty-six 1,000-lb (1-hour use) and thirty-six 500-lb (45-second use) plus sixty boxes of British incenliaries. Target Force BLUE needed eventy-two bombs but carried ighty-four, consisting of forty-eight ,000-lb (1-hour fuse) and thirty-six 00-lb (45-second fuse) bombs and hirty-six boxes of British incenliaries. Finally Target Force RED ad ninety-six bombs made up of orty-eight 1,000-lb (1-hour fuse) and orty-eight 500-lb (also 1-hour fuse) ombs, four short of the estimated umber to destroy this target, plus orty-eight clusters (two in each airraft) of American incendiaries. The wenty-three spare aircraft carried a otal of ninety-two 500-lb (45-second use) bombs and ninety-two clusters f American incendiaries. The 177 ircraft which successfully took off ally carried 818, made up of twenty-four 1,000-lb (1-6-hour fuse, totalling 24,000 lbs), thirty-six 500-lb (1-6-hour fuse, totalling 364,000 lbs), thirty-six 500-lb (1-6-hour fuse, totally 18,000 lbs), forty-eight 500-lb (1-hour fuse, totalling 24,000 lbs) and 386 500-lb (45-second fuse, totalling 193,000 lbs) 'demolition bombs,' plus 290 boxes of British and 140 clusters of American incendiaries.

By 0500 jeeps and trucks had deposited most crews at the dispersal points. Finally, at two minute intervals between 0600 and 0700, the heavily-laden bombers lumbered into the sky to commence circling in order to form squadron and group formations before setting out for the mission assembly line. At Terria excessive dust caused by the leading aircraft delayed take-off for planes still queuing at the head of the runway. Their delay proved wise, for one aircraft flying with the 98th turned back with engine trouble immediately after take-off, failed to locate the runway accurately through swirling dust and crashed, killing all but two of its crew. The dirty column of smoke which clawed skywards from this wreck made even the least superstitious uneasy.

Hence the two regular Ninth Air Force groups camouflaged in pinkish-brown and the three Eighth Air Force reinforcements with their dull green machines mustered 177 aircraft on the assembly line. Most aircraft carried nine or ten men, though some had eleven and one carried an unscheduled passenger – Rusty, a pet dog. 1,725 USAAF personnel set out, plus one RAF officer, Flight Lieutenant (later Squadron Leader) George C Barwell, who flew as top gunner with Major Norman C Appold of 376 Group. Sickness had caused several crew changes at a late hour, and nine of Colonel Kane's aircraft were actually manned by 389 Group crews. Major John J Jerstad, however, had no need to fly.

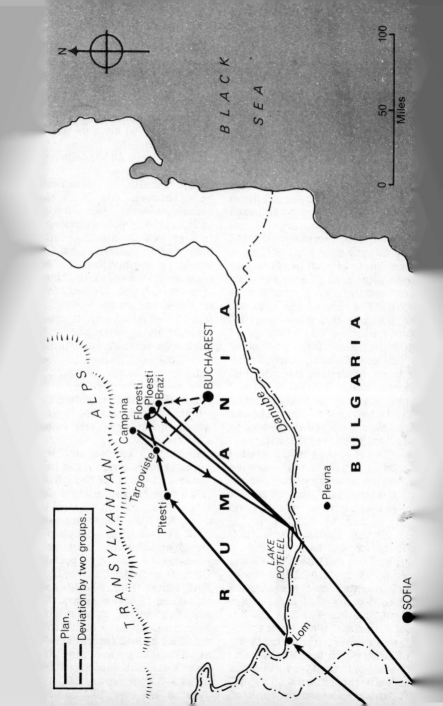

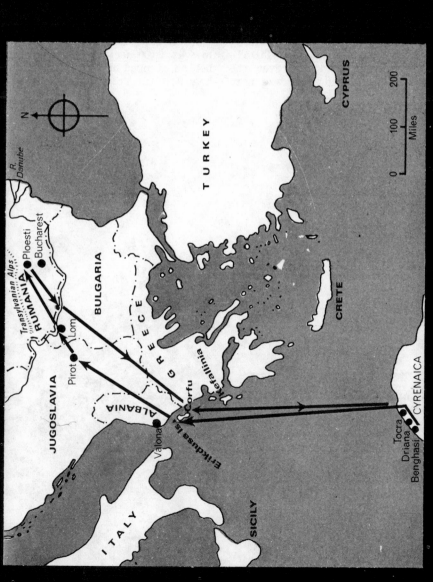

The plan of attack

One of those who had planned the details of TIDALWAVE, his tour of operations was finished and he required Brigadier-General Ent's permission to fly as Lieutenant Colonel Baker's co-pilot. Ent, himself the mission commander, wedged in a seat behind the two pilots, went in Captain Ralph P Thomson's aircraft of which Colonel Compton was co-pilot. Two important decisions were to be taken in this cockpit during the hours ahead.

Just after 0730 on that fateful Sunday, a slight haze still muffling the African coastline, the TIDALWAVE force headed out over the Mediterranean. Each group was more usually known by a nickname than its official numerical designation and individual aircraft also carried names, frequently illustrated with lurid designs, on the fuselage beneath the cockpit. Together with adjacent bomb symbols for completed missions and swastikas for enemy aircraft shot down, these imparted a personality to the B-24's inanimate mass of metal. It all helped to create a sense of crew solidarity, which comforted many men as the vast air armada got underway for Corfu 500 miles distant.

376 Group (The Liberandos) were low at 2,000 feet in the lead, and behind, stepped up according to plan, flew 93 (The Travelling Circus - so

named when Colonel Timberlake was its commander), 98 (The Pyramiders), 44 (The Flying Eightballs) and finally 389 (The Sky Scorpions) at 4,000 feet. Brigadier-General Ent's Field Order 58, issued from Headquarters Ninth Bomber Command on 28th July, noted that reliable information believed 'under 100' anti-aircraft guns were in the 'total refinery area', half only manned by Germans: specifically one two-gun position had been identified on the roof of the railway station (Ploesti South) adjacent to the Astra Romana refinery. Probably 'under 100 balloons . . . throughout the area' of the ordinary German type anchored by 2.7mm and 3mm cables: radar was set to

cover eastern approaches. The careful might just have noticed that amid these details Ent admitted 'no recent reports' of anti-aircraft and no detailed information on balloons. A comprehensive list of twenty-eight bases from the Levant through Egypt to Libya for use in case of emergency was appended, plus nine neutral Turkish airfields, the latter varying in altitude from Adana (58 feet) to Afyon (3,366 feet). Full details of length and direction of runway, precise coordinates, procedures for night landing and available medical facilities at these places were given. Seven of the Allied airfields would be on full standby, others available if required. Nothing had apparently been left to chance and justified the claim that: 'The implementation of the TIDAL-WAVE project is an outstanding example of the maximum utilisation of intelligence in planning'.

Ent's Field Order, the mission directive, laid down: 'The Ninth US Air Force will attack and destroy the seven principal oil refineries in the Ploesti area on 1st August 1943 employing seven target forces in a minimum altitude attack in order to deny the enemy use of the petroleum production processed in that area'. Colonel Kane's message to his Group was even more direct: 'We're going to knock out Ploesti or die trying'.

Once over the Mediterranean all haze cleared and the sun shone brightly, much to the discomfort of many crews who sweated profusely in their unpressurised cabins. The good visibility, however, enabled the groups easily to keep in visual contact 500 yards apart. Nevertheless, this part of the mission was not without incident, for, jettisoning their bombs and extra fuel onto the waves, ten abortives (seven from the 98th) turned for home. One specific, disturbing incident also took place. Contrary to Brigadier-General Ent's original in-

B-24s, aiming to 'knock out Ploesti or die trying'

117

tention, shortly before take-off Lieutenant Flavelle's *Wingo-Wango* had been detailed to lead the 376th and the entire mission force in place of Colonel Compton, who would fly further back in the formation. At approximately 1030 at the designated point south of Corfu, after three anxious hours and countless tedious miles over the ocean, the signal was given to climb to 10,000 feet. Failing to respond, Flavelle's aircraft instead slipped sideways, hit the sea and exploded with a total loss of life. Another incredulous pilot watched *Wingo Wango* 'stagger, dipping down and nosing up in ever-increasing movement, until its nose rose higher and higher into the air'. Ultimately it stood almost vertical on its tail then 'slid over on its back, and slowly gaining speed . . . dived violently into the sea'. This episode, which destroyed a second mission aircraft independent of enemy action was over in a matter of seconds. The plane carrying Brigadier-General Ent and Colonel Compton was out of visual contact with the leading element and, as radio silence was in force and Flavelle's deputy quickly took over the lead position, these two officers continued unaware of the tragedy. It is worth noting that the USAAF later officially recorded that Flavelle's loss had no 'special significance' concerning subsequent events.

With Corfu successfully negotiated and the required turn made over Erikousa, just after crossing the Albanian coast 'towering cumulus' from 10–15,000 feet and in places lower 'began to show above the mountains'. The summits of the Pindus Range running south-east from Albania to Greece and about 8,000 feet high were therefore uncomfortably close to the cloud base. Colonel Compton and Lieutenant-Colonel Baker decided to climb over the cloud, but Colonel Kane led his and the two following groups through it. This latter manoeuvre involved a complicated tactical procedure to avoid collisions, which

inevitably cost time. Considerable disorientation of formation had now occurred even within flights, but the most serious outcome of this action was that the leading two groups became separated from the trailing three and were also flying some way above them. Colonel Kane briefly regained visual sighting of the 93rd, but at this stage estimated the two leading groups to be thirty miles left of the correct course as well as too high.

200 miles from the Danube, over Jugoslavia, all semblance of mission unity was finally lost. Frequent rain squalls, which reduced visibility, were encountered, then another bank of cloud came into view. Penetration in safety seemed impossible, nor was circumvention apparently practicable. The simple decision therefore was whether to fly above or below it. The gap which had opened between the leading and trailing groups and the mandatory radio silence virtually ensured that no co-ordinated decision would be taken. The leading groups (376 and 93) in fact went above the cloud at 16,000 feet, the three trailing (98, 44 and 389) below at 10,000. Unfortunately a further natural freak served to hasten the disintegration of the route formation, for those flying high experienced strong following winds which carried them even further ahead of the others. When the cloud cleared after crossing the Osogvoska Range near the Jugoslav-Bulgarian border, the two high groups were utterly alone. But Brigadier-General Ent had no means of knowing this, nor that at this point the 98th was twenty minutes behind and trailing by some sixty miles. Only planes at the rear of 93 Group were aware of the serious situation that had developed.

Crossing the Danube at 1230 the leading groups headed for the First Initial Point, and soon the separation of the groups was to be exaggerated by another quirk of fate. When Colonel Kane began his descent after Pirot,

identified the Danube and saw no aircraft in front, he thought that he had
assumed the lead position of the
entire mission force. He therefore flew
westwards for some time to allow the
group behind him (which he believed
to be Colonel Compton's 376th followed by the 93rd) to pass ahead.
When the trailing group was identified
as the 44th, he resumed his onward
course, realising now the division
which had occurred. In effect TIDAL-
WAVE would not be carried out
simultaneously by five groups, but by
two task forces at different times:
the 376 and 93 Groups followed later by
98, 44 and 389. At about 1300 the latter
three set out for Pitesti from Lom, by
now almost a half an hour behind the
others.

Furthermore, events on the way
from the Adriatic had only underlined
the inability of such a large force to
escape detection and the futility of
maintaining a radio silence, which
might have prevented confusion of
the route formation, mounting of an
unco-ordinated attack on Ploesti and
much ultimate loss of life. As soon as
they entered Albanian airspace some
planes had been fired on by anti-
aircraft guns near Vlone, and through
the mountain mists of Albania and
Jugoslavia crews sighted mirrors and
torches flashing out the morse letter
'V'. In addition some airmen at
mission debriefing reported enemy
air activity over Bulgaria, which,
from later evidence, proved to be
ancient biplanes scrambled in fear of
an attack on Sofia, but too late to
catch the bombers as they flew on
northwards. The value of the pains-
taking preparation and training, all
the months of discussion and planning, was effectively lost over the
Macedonian hills. Presence of the
mission force had been divined long
before it reached the wheatlands of
Vallachia, and it was now too frag-
mented to compensate for detection
with efficient execution of its attack.
By the time that the Danube, dis-
appointingly murky and far from the

romantic blue of fiction, was crossed
two further abortives had reduced the
force to 164 aircraft and another B-24
was similarly to turn back before
Ploesti.

At 1330 the two leading groups
reached Pitesti, described officially as
'a nondescript small straggling town
situated at the confluence of two
valleys', where they dropped to minimum altitude, increased speed and
turned for Floresti. The contrast between pleasant Rumanian farmland,
arid African desert and the savage
mist-covered hills of Jugoslavia was
marked. The green countryside, with
its meandering streams, neat villages
and tree-lined roads seemed to many
of the aerial intruders a reproduction
of the American Middle West. People
could be clearly seen below and
several rustic dramas were visibly
enacted. One peasant woman, petrified
by the approaching monsters, crawled
under the hay cart she was leading.
The horses, however, displaying no
greater fortitude immediately bolted
to expose her face-downwards in the
dust. In another place a man leading
two horses abandoned his charges and
dived fully clothed into a stream.

Streams figured prominently in
reports of native reaction. Several
crews spoke of members of the oppo-
site sex bathing in one. The number
involved and their state of undress
escalated proportionately as the miles
away from Rumanian soil increased,
although ten crews insisted that a
single nude was involved. Substanti-
ated is the claim that over this idyllic
spot one crewman announced: 'Here's
where I bale out!', but the impression
that the lady in question stood up to
wave undoubtedly stemmed more
from hope than fact. Certainly another girl adopted a less welcoming
posture: in terror, she threw her
bright apron over her head. Elsewhere
farmers allegedly threw stones and
pitchforks at the aircraft, but an
elderly coupled reacted less belliger-
ently by falling on their knees in
prayer.

Above: A protective screen of light smoke envelopes the aiming points.
Below: Defensive smoke pots begin to operate

These incidents, some apocryphal and others embroidered, did not disturb the overall picture of peacefulness. As a result a sense of unreality, even euphoria, set in: 'just like the movies' . . . 'the prettiest country I've seen since the States' were among instinctive remarks. To many it all seemed unreal: no opposition, no hostile troops, waving people, beautiful girls. Some crews absorbed the atmosphere in silence, others chattered excitedly and a few burst into song. Extremes of feeling were illustrated when one crew rendered 'Don't Sit Under the Apple Tree' and another the doxology.

As the planes flew over wooded slopes towards Floresti joking tailed off and tension began to mount. Still no enemy activity; and hope rose that the mission was indeed undetected. Over Targoviste, so similar in situation to Floresti but twenty miles short of it, the first important decision – perhaps the more crucial – was taken in Colonel Compton's aircraft. Believing that the leading element had overshot the Second Initial Point and that this was actually Floresti, *Teggie Ann* broke radio silence, ordering pilots to turn down the valley below and adopt attack formation on 127 degrees beside the railway. Responsibility for this decision must lie with the mission commander, Brigadier-General Ent, but precisely who originally thought that Floresti lay below – Ent, Compton, Captain Thompson or the navigator – is not clear. Certainly it emerged later that the deputy lead navigator, who had assumed responsibility when *Wingo Wango* crashed, knew precisely where he was at that point.

Despite the number of similar valleys between the First and Second Initial Points and the variations in visibility due to sudden showers, it was immediately obvious that other crews also knew their exact position. Majors Appold and Potts were two pilots who quickly broke radio silence to point out the mistake and others

soon forcefully joined in. But with visibility reduced to six miles through haze, once committed to the turn Ent was virtually obliged to fly on in search of a positive point of recognition. Nine days after the raid Lieutenant-Colonel Forster bitterly wrote that Ent 'stupidly turned right at Targoviste, followed the railway to Bucharest, and ignoring all my written and verbal instructions to cross this railway and continue along the line of the oilfields to Floresti, observing several unmistakeable landmarks en route'. Such observations were easily made from Africa.

According to plan the two groups now divided into three target forces heading for WHITE 1, 2 and 3. As they flew south-eastwards flak began to open up and the extra forward-pointing guns in the leading aircraft were brought into play. One pilot reported: 'I saw fifty-calibre slugs churning up dust, spewing sparks off the gun barrels, and soldiers frantically running'. No fighters appeared and no aircraft had yet been shot down, as the target forces flew on at over 200mph (some 50mph faster than the average route speed) ostensibly towards their own targets.

When the spires of Bucharest appeared ahead, Ent ordered the aircraft to turn due north. Ent must have known long before this that he had made a wrong turn because the attack run from Floresti to Ploesti would only have taken four minutes. Targoviste to Bucharest took almost fifteen minutes and it is therefore probable that in the reduced visibility that Ent was waiting for a definite navigational fix before deciding on another change of course. This new course would bring the aircraft to Ploesti from the south, not north-west as practised. But what precisely Ent had in mind is still uncertain, though some pilots believed that they were flying back to find Floresti. As the planes made their unscheduled turn, Rumanian IAR-80s attacked the rear elements. In *Jersey Bounce* the rear gunner, Sergeant

Another successful hit during the 389th Group's attack

Leycester D Havens, was killed – perhaps the first TIDALWAVE airman to die through enemy action. The leading two groups were now approaching Ploesti from an entirely unfamiliar angle and in the fourteen minutes flight from Bucharest encountered all manner of anti-aircraft opposition. Haystacks and wagons in railway sidings fell apart to reveal blazing 88mm guns, smaller calibre weapons opened up from concrete positions and flak towers, even infantry loosed off their small arms. In the smoke and confusion three aircraft went down, as the mission leader tried desperately to identify landmarks. So intense was enemy fire that south of the town Compton turned east, possibly to reach either the Initial Point or his own isolated Romana Americana target outside of the inner ring of flak. 'Several miles' later, according to him, the 376th turned north then west, but 'in the vicinity' of its target Brigadier-General Ent decided that the defences were now so thoroughly alerted that the TIDALWAVE plan to attack WHITE 1 could not be effected: group reports later mentioned 'intense light anti-aircraft and machine-gun fire . . . in circling the target', which caused some 200 holes in one aircraft. At almost precisely 1400 Ent made his second important decision and ordered the 376th to attack targets of opportunity: incredibly at virtually the same moment, with the 376th having bombed no target and without news of the other four groups, he also sent two morse letters to Benghasi – 'MS' (Mission Successful). Many 376th aircraft released their bombs on tank cars in nearby marshalling yards, others peeled off to bomb oil wells and their adjacent storage tanks northeast of the town; but some simply jettisoned their bombs over fields or woods.

The 376th had in fact flown over the Credituel Minier refinery at Brazi on its way north from Bucharest and one south of the southern Ploesti refineries after its eastwards turn. Its subsequent manoeuvres carried it round its own target (presumably unidentifiable in the heat of battle) to the east and Ent's order to abandon the mission plan was given when north-east of Ploesti following a twenty mile detour of the town. After receiving this order and dropping their bombs 'the major portion' of the 376th officially flew northwards 'beyond Campina' to escape the hail of anti-aircraft fire, by-passing the refinery there 'just a few minutes' before the 389th arrived. Then it turned south towards home. One element led by Major Appold (Colonel Smart later insisted that Appold led six not three planes in this enterprise) neither jettisoned its bombs nor flew towards Campina, but approached Ploesti from the north-east. Five minutes after Ent's order Appold's three, dodging chimneys and flak and flying at 120–250 feet, attacked WHITE 2. As the designated target force of the 93rd was never to reach this target, Concordia Vega would have escaped unscathed without Appold's action. Of his attack, Appold reported: 'It was the damnedest thing ever. While civilians in the streets waved at us, gunners on the house tops were shooting at us'. One of his gunners, the RAF officer Barwell, later commented that as an explosion on the ground threw the aircraft sideways he had 'the unique experience for a top gunner of seeing our bombs alongside, still falling. They crashed into a large cracking plant'. As the aircraft entered the smoke and chaos a moment of panic chilled this crew, then choking fumes filled the aircraft. Fortunately this proved to be smoke from chimneys which had penetrated the perforated fuselage and it soon cleared. Apart from Appold's effort the twenty-six aircraft of the 376th which reached Ploesti hit no planned target: the group lost only one aircraft in action, as approached by 8–10 enemy fighters which made 'uneager attacks' and claimed one Me-109 destroyed. Dummy oil installations were reported by it south-east and north-west of Ploesti.

Immediate post-raid claims by the group were a considerable exaggeration of fact. In 'poor visibility' because of haze and showers, hits were reported on the distillation plants and fractionating tower of Astra Romana. This is extremely unlikely. To reach this target from the point at which Brigadier-General Ent gave licence to attack targets of opportunity would have entailed a south-westerly course of approximately five miles across the whole width of Ploesti on a collision course with the 93rd – at that precise time attacking Astra Romana. The claim of damage to the fractionating tower at Concordia Vega by Appold's element was later confirmed, however. As the Group departed it noted that the 'entire Ploesti area appeared on fire'. If so, it was little due to its efforts.

Meanwhile Lieutenant - Colonel Baker's 93rd Group destined for WHITE 2 and 3 had followed the 376th after the erroneous turn at Targoviste and also altered course north short of Bucharest to approach Ploesti from an unrehearsed direction. During the northwards flight to Ploesti crew members reported numerous anti-aircraft positions, sightings of gunners desperately trying to reach safety or man their weapons as the B-24s approached and balloons, previously anchored, being belatedly put up. When the 376th turned east to skirt south of Ploesti, Baker 'chose' to attack refineries immediately to his front, which had now come into view. These were WHITE 4 (Astra Romana) and WHITE 5 (Colombia Aquila) on the southern edge of Ploesti, which had been allocated to 98 and 44 Groups. At this time, about 1345, haze and intermittent showers reduced visibility (seven-tenths cumulus at 5,000 feet and thundery outbreaks of rain were reported), which a quarter of an hour later had improved considerably when the targets were eventually attacked by their despatched target forces. Although some crews claimed to have hit WHITE 2 (Concordia Vega) and WHITE 3 (Standard Petrol Block and Unirea Sperantza), no damage at all was sustained by the latter.

After five abortives, thirty-two out of thirty-seven 93rd Group aircraft reached the target area, but one succumbed to anti-aircraft fire just short of Ploesti. Between 1350 and 1400 attacks were carried out at 100–300 feet on Targets WHITE 4 and 5. Considerable flak was experienced and several enemy fighters were reported, of which one Me-109 and one Fw-190 were claimed destroyed. Six to ten balloons appeared south of Ploesti at 3,000 feet, the heavy flak was considered 'for the most part inaccurate', the light flak 'of moderate intensity' and some machine-guns close to the targets of little consequence. Good camouflage of the gun batteries was, however, apparent. The 93rd reported that some smoke pots began belatedly to act, but the main problem came from the billowing oil of exploding tanks. Despite such undemonstrative accounts of anti-aircraft activity, eleven B-24s were lost in the target area, almost all to flak gunners.

On the approach to Ploesti one aircraft certainly struck a balloon cable and exploded, but another severed a cable without losing height or momentum. Several planes were hit by roof-top gunners in the town. One aircraft performed like a movie stunt machine, flying in one side of a large building and out the other side in flames and without wings, before exploding in mid-air. A few parachutes were seen to come out of stricken machines and from others, like *Pudgy* and *Honky-Tonk Gal*, men escaped once the planes had crash-landed. The unrehearsed target approach and further division of the 376th and 93rd was undoubtedly responsible for much of the aerial tumult which developed. As one pilot put it: 'Flights of three or four, or single planes, were flying in different directions, streaking smoke and flames, striking the ground, wings, tails and fuselages breaking up, big balls of smoke rolling out of the wrecks before they stopped shuddering'. The situation was so confused that no totally accurate sequence of the events may ever be known. The Duke of Wellington once likened a battle to a ball: you could later recall the identity of your partners but never the order in which you danced with them. In another century and another dimension of war, the battle of Ploesti confirmed this judgement.

Some Target Force WHITE 3 aircraft claimed to have hit their assigned Aiming Points, but this is unlikely. What is certain, however is that Lieutenant-Colonel Baker himself perished and another plane demolished the Ploesti women's prison in a spectacular eruption. Three miles south of Ploesti *Hell's Wench* (with Baker and Major Jerstad at the controls) was hit by flak in the nose and a fierce fire started. Baker might have made a belly-landing at this point, but continued to lead the 93rd towards the target that he had chosen. Lieutenant Walter T Stewart the deputy group leader in *Utah Man* the only aircraft which survived on Target Force WHITE 2's lead flight saw *Hell's Wench* continue steadily into the target area as flames gradually engulfed the superstructure and shudder as more anti-aircraft shells rapped its disintegrating frame. Only after leading the following B-24s through the refinery and dropping its own bombs (almost certainly on Target WHITE 5) did the lead aircraft, by now a virtual funeral pyre, pull up its nose in an attempt to gain height for the crew to bale out. The attempt effectively failed. Although the aircraft wobbled to 300 feet and three or four parachutes came out, none of the crew lived. Stewart believed that, considering the state of *Hell's Wench*, the combined strength of both pilots would have been necessary to pull the aircraft's nose up for the escape attempt. Both Baker and Jerstad received posthumous Congressional Medals of Honour 'for conspicuous gallantry and intrepidity above and beyond the call of duty'.

In the meantime, having realised over the Danube that the two leading groups must be ahead, Colonel Kane set out at approximately 1300 for Pitesti, where three quarters of an hour later the 389th altered course for Campina. The 98th and 44th then flew on towards Floresti, which they reached without difficulty, possibly because visibility in the area of Targoviste had now considerably improved. At this stage, because of the false turn of the two leading groups, they had effectively halved to fifteen minutes the gap between the two parts of the mission force. But, as Colonels Kane and Johnson were following the TIDALWAVE plan, the four groups destined for Ploesti and Brazi were approaching on a collision course. Fortunately this would never result in disaster, as the 98th and 44th reached Floresti just after the 93rd finished its bombing run.

At Floresti the two groups deployed into attack formation with Kane's Target Force WHITE 4 (Astra Romana and Unirea Orion) on the left, in the centre Colonel Johnson heading for WHITE 5 (Columbia Aquila) and on the extreme right, on an individual course and separated from the other two by the railway, were Lieutenant-Colonel Posey's aircraft aiming for Brazi and the Credituel Minier refinery (Target BLUE). Some reports suggest that only Kane was left of the railway and Johnson and Posey both to its right. This appears most improbable, in view of the different heading of Posey's force and the details of the TIDALWAVE plan which Kane and Johnson otherwise followed faithfully.

As they flew the thirteen miles from Floresti to Ploesti Target Forces WHITE 4 and 5 were met by flak, alerted by previous events south of the town: this proved particularly effective when 88mm guns on the slopes of the valley opened up a crossfire. The additional forward-pointing .50 machine-guns were only partially effective as they sprayed the ground up to a mile ahead of the bombers. In one respect these two target forces were particularly unfortunate. On the railway track between Ploesti and Floresti was an armoured train, especially equipped for anti-aircraft action. This certainly caused an enormous amount of damage to the low-flying aircraft already committed to their attack formation. Its appearance on that line was later found to result from enemy knowledge of the approaching bombers derived from his own detection systems. But at the time wild rumours about betrayal of the mission were rife. Apart from the train, ground-based flak and the inevitable small-arms fire, the B-24s had to contend with bombing from above by Ju-87 Stukas and the intermittent attention of German and Rumanian fighters, whose activities were mercifully restricted by the energy of their own flak gunners.

During this approach to the target Kane noted 'several' desert-coloured B-24s passing below him in a south-westerly direction. The timing of this sighting and other similar reports suggests that Kane was referring to Major Appold's element of the 376th, which was leaving Concordia Vega as Kane approached from Floresti. But more than three aircraft were apparently seen, which may support Colonel Smart's contention that more aircraft attacked WHITE 2. A further point is raised by this incident. Officially 'the major portion' of the 376th flew north to the Campina area after Ent's order to bomb independently; but later the 389th reported 'one squadron' of the 376th approaching as it bombed. Undoubtedly some 376th aircraft had already left the Campina area by this

Above: Target White 4 during the bombardment by Colonel John R Kane's 98th Group. *Below right and below left:* Firefighting efforts at Ploesti refineries

ime, but there remains a suspicion
hat rather more pilots than Appold
ither did bomb in Ploesti or took a
horter route home.

Thirty-nine of the forty-six 98
Group aircraft that had set out led by
Colonel Kane in *Hail Columbia* were
ow heading for WHITE 4. One hit a
balloon and touched off its explosive
charge with fatal consequences; an-
ther, having been damaged by guns
rom the armoured train, was shot
own by a lurking Me-109. Several
irtually disintegrated in the air,
vith few parachutes successfully
merging. One pilot reported: 'The
nti-aircraft made good with six
irect hits on my ship . . . [which
estroyed] my hydraulics, oxygen,
lectricity and radio,' thus persuading
im that 'closest to the ground was
afest'. He eventually got back to
frica, but of the six aircraft in the
fth wave which attacked this target
nly one emerged airborne. So heavy
vas the flak that one airman claimed:
They hit us with everything but

Colonel Leon W Johnson's B-24s
approach their target White 5,
previously damaged by 93rd Group

bricks'. Later Lieutenant Royden L
Lebrecht thought the previous attacks by the 93rd on the target 'unfortunate . . .[and] mainly responsible
for the losses of the 98th Bombardment Group'.

Kane himself was appalled at the
shambles he found at Ploesti, where
twenty-one of his aircraft were lost:
'We expected to take losses but I will
never forget those big Liberators
going down like flies'. Another officer
reported: 'I looked out of the side
windows and saw the others flying
through smoke and flames'; in the
event Colonel Kane's arms were
singed by the heat over the target.
With certainty two aircraft exploded
above the refinery and one belly-
landed nearby as a result of flak
damage. Another B-24 was also lost at
this time when six Me-109s and three
twin-engined aircraft attacked the

Group coming away from the target.

Like Kane, Colonel Johnson's Target Force WHITE 5 had to attack a refinery already thoroughly alerted and damaged by the 93rd Group some fifteen minutes earlier. Both Target Forces WHITE 4 and 5 attacked from 1405 to 1415 at 120–250 feet, but faced exploding bombs from the previous attacks and the black clouds of burning oil which obscured perilous chimneys and balloon cables – two aircraft were downed by the latter. Just before Johnson's aircraft *Suzy Q* bombed, a refinery installation erupted: Johnson's veteran plane survived but two, possibly three, others did not in the blast of similar explosions. Later the Colonel said: 'It was the closest thing to Dante's Inferno I've seen'. *K for King* emerged from the holocaust with a huge gap in the fuselage, part of one stabilising fin gone and a feathered engine, but survived to reach its home base. Following crews saw two aircraft in one flight simultaneously shatter into a thousand parts and another hit the ground apparently sent out of control by the dreaded prop-wash. One plane limped on with two feathered engines, another cripple was pursued by an Me-109 which needed to put its flaps down to avoid overshooting its prey. Of this doomed B-24 a gunner remarked: 'There wasn't much left of our plane but daylight.' From Johnson's target force five aircraft were lost over Ploesti and the Colonel's own commentary on the whole experience seems apt. 'It's indescribable to anyone who wasn't there'.

Airmen who crashed and survived had a variety of experiences on the ground. Some later reported being robbed by peasants as they lay dazed and wounded, others spoke of Rumanian civilians keeping back German soldiers until the arrival of their own troops. One crew was cared for by Rumanian women who soothed their wounds with a locally-made balm and another airman recalled receiving a refreshing drink of milk in the shade of a tree from a farm-girl as she leaned

over a fence.

Target Force BLUE, the 44th Group's other aircraft led by Lieutenant-Colonel Posey, had considerabl[e] trouble with enemy fighters, but di[d] not lose a single aircraft over th[e] target. Following its own course from Floresti it was too far west to be hi[t] by the flak train. Seventy-five mile[s] south of Ploesti one of Posey's B-24[s] claimed to have shot down an Me-11[0] by squirting it from beneath with it[s] extra forward guns, and indeed a[s] Posey's aircraft left the target are[a] they were heavily attacked. On[e] aircraft crashed with a total loss o[f] life, and there was little consolatio[n] that in its death throes it shot dow[n] the tormenting Me-109. The accurac[y] of Posey's force, however, achieve[d] the best results of the whole TIDAL WAVE mission. Attacking betwee[n] 1410 and 1415 at 120–250 feet it droppe[d] its bombs unhindered by the spars[e] smoke screen and high strato[-] cumulus cloud. Of the eighteen t[o] twenty enemy aircraft which at[-] tacked, mainly after the targe[t] thirteen were claimed as destroye[d] and one damaged.

As planned and virtually simultan[e-] eously with the attack of the 98th an[d] 44th, Colonel Jack Wood's 389 Grou[p] bombed Steaua Romana (Target RE[D] at Campina between 1410 and 1420 a[t] 200–700 feet. The approach to th[e] target, however, was not entirel[y] smooth. Leaving Colonels Kane an[d] Johnson at Pitesti, the 389th followe[d] a north-easterly course at 4,000 fee[t] over the hills. RED Target was situ[-] ated in a valley three miles wid[e] which sloped towards the south-eas[t] and the plan was to attack from [a] north-westerly direction. As furthe[r] south in the Targoviste regio[n] several similar valleys existed in th[e] foothills of the Transylvanian Alp[s] Wood (in Captain Caldwell's aircraf[t] like Brigadier-General Ent on a stoo[l] behind the two pilots) was to f[ly] north up the next valley to that con[-] taining Campina, quickly clear th[e] intervening ridge at a point betwee[n]

Sinaia and Campina and turn down the attack valley to the target. Like Ent, Colonel Wood found that, despite endless rehearsals, the similarity of the valleys was confusing and, moreover, mist hanging over neighbouring summits obscured prominent landmarks – crucially in his case a prominent monastery. He therefore turned north up what he thought was the penultimate valley, hopped the ridge and found there was one more to go. His whole force then made a 180-degree turn within the narrow confines of this valley without loss, flew north again, hopped another ridge and this time was able to attack down the right valley. This manoeuvre was a tribute to efficiency and discipline, for some pilots realised that Wood's initial turn was a mistake, but neither broke radio silence nor took individual action by continuing eastwards. So the entire force was able to get on course again, retain its planned order of attack and reach the target without loss. Campina was a compact collection of neat single-storeyed buildings interspersed with tree-lined streets. The oil refinery stood on the edge of the town, which was surrounded by fallow fields sloping upwards towards rolling hills in the distance. On this beautiful August afternoon it seemed lazily peaceful as the crews approached. The scene ahead fitted in with the family outings, groups of horsemen and parties of picnickers that had been spotted already below. The post-raid report recorded that 'peasants in fields and streets waved hands and shovels etc'. 'Numerous hits on all four divisions' of the diamond-shaped target (a mere 100 feet wide at one point) were recorded with bombs dropped by the quick toggle method at ten to twenty-foot intervals in clear weather. Accurate light anti-aircraft and machine-gun fire was reported (two aircraft being hit by machine-guns and two having engines damaged by flak), three to six enemy aircraft encountered (of which an Me-109 and Me-110

were claimed destroyed): Lieutenant-Colonel Forster later described the 389th's attack as 'a howling success'.

To discourage fighter interference and avoid the heavy flak guns which might be unable to depress, the 389th actually went down lower after the target for some forty minutes. One officer said later: 'High-altitude bombing is much better. At 100 feet you see too damn much and besides being hard on your nerves . . . it scares hell out of you'. This Group flew further than the others and another officer complained: 'We were so long over enemy territory that we felt like taking out citizenship papers'.

One of Wood's aircraft was caught in the explosion of a boilerhouse, which had been hit by a previous aircraft, and Second Lieutenant Lloyd H Hughes' B-24 was struck by machine-gun fire in fuel tanks during the approach run down the valley. Over the target fuel pouring from the holed tanks was ignited and the fiery mass was then steered by the pilot towards a dry river-bed. Here some semblance of a landing was achieved amid a shower of disintegrating fuselage and burning tanks. The citation for the subsequent award of a posthumous Congressional Medal of Honour to Hughes drew attention to the fact that he could have force-landed in any of a number of cornfields before entering 'the target area (which) was blazing with burning oil tanks and damaged refinery installations from which flames leaped high above the bombing level of the formation'. Knowing the danger of entering such a conflagration with escaping fuel he nevertheless flew over the target, dropped his bombs and only then attempted to land his now-blazing aircraft. Hughes' actions were 'gallant and valorous' and he risked his life 'above and beyond the call of duty'. Only three men came out of the wreck and one of these later died.

In addition to this loss and the aircraft cremated over the exploding boilerhouse, four other 389th planes

A low-flying B-24 over target

went down in the target area. From one only the top-turret gunner survived. Others saw the plane crash in flames; the gunner continued to fire a few bursts, then a figure broke out of the plexiglass dome and dashed for safety through the smoke. In all, three B-24s crashed just south of Campina. Ten minutes after the target two parachutes came out of another which actually continued on its way and twenty minutes later one B-24 turned east in search of neutral Turkey with one engine smoking. Incredibly one aircraft, *Shoot Fritz You're Faded*, came down on the estate of a Rumanian princess at Nedelea, ten miles north-west of Ploesti, with the loss only of the flight engineer. Three of the survivors were then sumptuously entertained at the stately home. Members of this crew witnessed at close range the antipathy which existed between the Rumanians and their German allies, when a veritable tug-of-war took place for possession of their persons. This incident also suggested another interesting factor. One of the princess's retainers reported that a Russian aircraft had crashed, pointing to the white star ringed with red (later red was removed from the official American aircraft insignia). It is therefore possible that, bearing in mind their traditional hatred of Russia, Rumanians threw stones and other handy missiles at the B-24s in the belief that they were repelling emissaries from Moscow.

The piecemeal assaults on Ploesti, Campina and Brazi between 1350 and 1420 ensured that plans for a general rally at Lake Balta Potelel and an orderly withdrawal via the Adriatic Sea would be still-born. By 1445 aircraft were scattered throughout the Wallachian Plain travelling at different speeds and altitudes in various states of disrepair. Apart from shortage of fuel, the attention of virulent fighters (principally Me-109s and IAR-80s; but Me-110, Fw-190, Ju-88, Ju-87, Do-217, He-112, He-113, and Italian Mc-202 sightings were reported

plus a motley collection of biplanes) discouraged leading survivors from waiting for those behind. All planes, some as low as twenty feet, hugged the ground to avoid fighters after the target area: some returned to base with grass and hay clinging to the fuselage and the bomb-bay doors of one were reputedly amputated by a fence. The low altitude adopted caused at least one enemy aircraft to go nose first into the ground, unable to pull out of its dive. Recalling this phenomenon with relish one observer remarked: 'Those fighters used non-habit-forming tactics'. Colonel Johnson in Major Brandon's *Suzy Q*, an elderly machine which had come through many misfortunes in the past and at one time had been fitted with four entirely new engines, was to reach Benina with Captain William R Cameron's *Buzzin' Bear* after thirteen hours forty minutes in the air. These were the only two aircraft of 44 Group's 66th and 67th Bombardment Squadrons to get home that day. Lieutenant Stewart's *Utah Man* of 93 Group arrived at Terria fourteen hours after departure, displaying some 365 fuselage holes; and the last B-24 to reach home after a sixteen hour flight was Lieutenant Kenton D McFarland's *Liberty Lad*, which limped in with two engines dead, minus hydraulic power and without lights on the instrument panel in pitch darkness. Understandably the two pilots took some days to recover.

Crippled aircraft were particularly vulnerable, for others could rarely afford to throttle down to protect them for fear of running out of fuel later. Hence to feather an engine was, in the opinion of an Eighth Air Force officer, 'like writing the boys at the mortuary for space on their slab'. The slower B-24s, some managing a mere 120mph, in particular attracted the twin-engined Ju-88s, which were less able to cope with faster aircraft. As they withdrew from the target area pilots had to choose between the planned route via Bulgaria, Jugoslavia and

Greece to Corfu, Corfu in European Turkey, Turkish bases across the Bosphorus or Cyprus. The latter three courses would all involve a lengthy time over Bulgaria and that to Cyprus a 500-mile violation of Turkish airspace as well. Two damaged aircraft that did make for Cyprus had to decline persistent invitations from Turkish American-built P-40 Warhawks to land in Turkey. Several other pilots did also successfully land in Turkey and Cyprus, including Colonel Kane. He survived a hair-raising trip, in which *Hail Columbia* with one engine dead and another damaged crawled over the Balkan mountain peaks, which rise to over 9,000 feet, to reach Nicosia and dine that night in a Cypriot night club.

The 376th and 389th were the least-damaged groups and most of their remaining aircraft did pick up some sort of protective formation for the planned homeward run via Corfu; but the two groups flew about thirty minutes apart in separate formations. The bulk of the residue in 98 and 44 Groups also followed the planned route, though they did combine. This return route which took the B-24s closer to Sofia than the outward journey gave the Bulgarians opportunity to intervene. At its debriefing one 98 Group crew commented that attacks by Bulgarian biplanes south of the Danube 'caused much needed merriment,' but, although they were too slow to make more than one pass, the Avias certainly caused considerable trouble for some battle-weary crews. North-west of Pleven a number attacked, damaging two engines of one B-24 and making more superficial holes in others. West of Sofia Me-109s from Karlovo also appeared to account for two B-24s. From one of these only a single gunner survived by kicking his way out of the tail position as the doomed aircraft spiralled earthwards in flames: four from the other escaped into Jugoslavia after a pancake landing near the border, where they joined up with local partisans.

Several fleeing aircraft made skilful use of cloud cover to escape enemy fighters, but for two this haven proved disastrous. Flying through cloud *Let 'Er Rip* and *Exterminator* collided, killing all but three from the combined crews. However, humour was not altogether absent from this part of the flight. At one stage a figure clad in voluminous, coloured underwear dashed from his farmhouse to discharge an ancient shotgun at the passing bombers, and one 389th aircraft flew straight through a haystack to emerge bespattered but unscathed. Over the mountains of Jugoslavia and Greece the cloud had thickened with cumulus up to 30–40,000 feet, but it proved possible to penetrate this at 15,000 feet. Shortly before 1730, over the Ionian Sea west of the island of *Kefallinia*, when fears of enemy interference had receded if not vanished and many gunners had used up their ammunition, Me-109s and Fw-190s from the Greek mainland attacked the 98th and 44th remnants out of the sun, in what was officially termed 'a most unfortunate interception'. For about half an hour the enemy attacked both in waves and singly from many different directions, until forced to break off through lack of fuel. Four B-24s were lost during this episode. The crew of one was picked up from life rafts by Italians, seven of another which ditched west of Crete survived thirty hours in the Mediterranean before being rescued by an RAF launch from Cyprus. After this final brush with the enemy some damaged planes were obliged to make for Malta or Sicily.

Back at the North African bases, where few officially knew details of TIDALWAVE, it had been a long day. All mission days were a strain for anxious ground staff unable to do more than wait, but the special desert practice, new Eighth Air Force reinforcements and several modifications to equipment suggested that this was a special raid. As the hours went by far beyond the length of a normal mission, speculation mounted. At 1400 (1500 local time),when the aircraft were actually over the target,section leaders at Headquarters Ninth Bomber Command were told details of the mission and, during this meeting, Brigadier-General Ent's 'MS' (Mission Successful) was received.

Towards 1900 (2000 local time) tension began to rise and twenty minutes later the first B-24 returned as the sun was setting. By 1945 fifteen (all damaged) had reached Terria; a quarter of an hour later only eighteen of the 98th Group departures had

Returned Liberator of the 376th Group; only one of their aircraft was lost in action

The first B-24s return to base after the mission

returned and twenty-three from 44th Group's thirty-seven. When darkness fell at 2010 many remained unaccounted for and, although some, like *Liberty Lad*, were yet to arrive safely, by midnight about seventy aircraft were still missing. Some of these, unbeknown to Benghasi, had reached remote friendly bases or neutral Turkey. But some, like those destroyed in the Ionian Sea, had foundered on the very brink of safety. One was *Hadley's Harem*. This cripple flew with Colonel Kane via Bulgaria in an attempt to reach Cyprus. Over the Gulf of Antalya its remaining two engines faltered and the pilot turned

back for a crash-landing on the Turkish shore. The stricken plane hit the water a half a mile short of land and sank almost immediately. With the escape hatches jammed, seven of the crew managed to beat their way out through the walls of the shell-ridden fuselage as the waters closed over them. Neither pilot was one of these. Ultimately the survivors reached the beach exhausted and were cared for through the night by sympathetic fishermen. Later, after protracted negotiations based on the claim that they were shipwrecked mariners not belligerents liable to internment, an Air-Sea Rescue launch took them to Cyprus.

During the night of 1st-2nd August raid photographs taken by the cameras in the B-24s were developed, the wounded received attention and the weary rest. On the morrow an inquest would commence in earnest. The man whose actions must inevitably come under the closest scrutiny was Brigadier-General Ent. Earlier, after landing at Berka 2, Flight Lieutenant Barwell had noted the gloom which pervaded a group discussion between Ent, Colonel Compton and Major-General Brereton. He commented to his pilot: 'I am really quite sorry for General Ent. He's one of the best of your chaps I've met'. Possibly through his decisions over Rumania that day, however, many men had died and the mission's success had been placed in jeopardy. At the post-raid debriefing, hollow-eyed and exhausted, an officer of 44 Group was asked for his impression of the mission. His reply described TIDAL-WAVE for most participants: 'We were dragged through the mouth of Hell'.

Brigadier-General Ent, right, and Colonel Compton, centre, in front of the 'Liberandos' which carried them on the raid

Counting the cost

Survivors later recalled with enthusiasm their impressions of TIDALWAVE: 'The Ploesti mission was the biggest thing I was ever on'; 'I just returned from one of the most daring raids yet made in this war'; 'It was the most exciting raid I've been on so far'. In losses, however, it was decidedly costly.

Early on 2nd August a Ninth Air Force summary reported that ninety-six aircraft had returned to the Benghasi area, ten were known to have reached Cyprus, four Sicily, four Malta and one Turkey. Twenty losses in action were confirmed, one had

been lost en route (*Wingo Wango*), thirteen had aborted, which left twenty-nine unaccounted for at this stage. During the day unofficial reports from Turkey stated that four B-24s had landed in the Izweim area, four others in Thrace. That evening the British Air Attaché in Ankara signalled more reliable information. The Turkish government confirmed that four aircraft had landed at Corlu and one at Gazbairmir with the crews safe, one at Cardak about which there were no details and one near Torbali,

Debriefing of pilots after a mission

outh of Izmir, in a state of considerable disrepair with the pilot dead and
two crew members wounded . Another
Hadley's Harem) had crashed in the
sea off Manavgat for the loss of three
lives.

Gradually more news filtered
through to Headquarters Ninth Bomber Command, and more aircraft
reached their home bases after emergency landings on 1st August and
overnight stops at other airfields. The
final total of loss and damage made
depressing reading, for in the end only
41 returned and over 50 per cent of
these were damaged. From 178 aircraft
which took to the air forty-one were
lost in action – 376th (1), 93rd (11),
98th (18), 44th (7), 389th (4). Eight
others, including *Hadley's Harem*,
were in Turkey and therefore effectively lost and five had crashed
through 'miscellaneous causes' – one
en route, one on take-off, one in
Cyprus and two into the sea on the
way back. Fifty-four B-24s were therefore lost and another fifty-eight
classified as 'damaged', which did not
include more lightly affected machines. The actual losses were remarkably close to those claimed by the
Luftwaffe, which estimated forty-
eight shot down and fifty-five 'severely
damaged'. These were considerably
more realistic than American claims
of fifty-one enemy losses. Afterwards
American intelligence authorities admitted a report from a 'usually
reliable' agent in Rumania that four
German and eight Rumanian fighters
were lost, twenty damaged. Subsequent data established with certainty
that two Me-109s from Zilistea and
two Me-109s from Mizil were lost, plus
two Me-109s by Luftwaffe units engaged in the battle over the Ionian
Sea. But no reliable figures for
Rumanian and Bulgarian losses are
available.

Of the TIDALWAVE groups the
93th lost twenty-one aircraft
(eighteen in combat), the 44th eleven
(seven in combat), the three Eighth
Air Force groups lost thirty out of

their ninety-eight attacking aircraft,
although six of these did reach Turkey. In manpower alone the American
losses were daunting. Including the
aircraft which crashed on take-off,
the fifty-four lost B-24s contained
542 men. Two survived the initial
crash, seven were saved from *Hadley's
Harem* and subsequently brought to
Cyprus. A further ten were rescued
from the aircraft which crash-landed
in Cyprus on the return flight. Effectively therefore 523 airmen were lost,
but to these must be added the fifty or
so wounded who died or were disabled
by their wounds after successfully
reaching North Africa. In all, seventy-
five men were interned in Turkey, but
following the release of the seven survivors of *Hadley's Harem* the Turks
failed to keep an effective watch on
the remainder. Conveniently they
'escaped' to the coast, where RAF
launches arrived surreptitiously at
night to transport them to friendly
Cyprus. Like the Halpro internees
these men ultimately returned to
service, leaving their machines in
captivity.

Some 150 men were made prisoners
of war in Rumania and Bulgaria. A
few did make for the Transylvanian
Alps as advised, but were defeated by
their inability to converse in the
native language or by sheer bad luck.
Many were well-treated, especially
those who stayed in Rumanian hands:
at the time a former British Minister
in Bucharest estimated that 80 per
cent of Rumanians were pro-British.
The reason for the comparatively
friendly reception given to American
captives was more probably war
weariness (after about half a million
casualties in action), accentuated by
German arrogance and a realisation
that, following their defeat at Stalingrad, the Germans were likely to
leave Rumania in the foreseeable
future. In view of traditional antipathy towards the USSR, pro-Ameri-
can demonstrations of friendship may
therefore have been tinged with a
certain political expediency.

A B-24 complete with map indicating raids on Ploesti

Lieutenant John D Palm, whose leg was severely damaged when *Brewery Wagon* crashed, had the limb skillfully amputated and later received sympathetic visits from the Rumanian King and the Queen Mother. Other wounded were treated principally at Bucharest and Sinaia, and the fit in Rumania were initially housed in the Bucharest gaol. Ultimately, except for the few who were permanently hospitalised, the American prisoners were taken up the Campina valley and through the Predeal Pass to the ski resort of Timisul de Jos. Here they were placed in a camp, where at first condi-

tions were not unpleasant, apart from the primitive plumbing which remained as a testimony to pre-war French influence, and regular deliveries of Red Cross parcels were allowed. Some hopefuls made escape attempts and actually managed a few days of freedom. Ultimately conditions in the camp deteriorated, when Allied air action was resumed with more ferocity and greater success in April 1944. At length most American prisoners of war were snatched to safety in a bizarre rescue operation by Fifteenth Air Force planes from Italy in September 1944. After the Rumanians had first concluded an armistice with the USSR, then declared war against Germany, the Germans bombed and closed in on

claimed thirty-six aircraft destroyed and sixty-six airmen captured, and also noted eight bombers 'forced down' in Turkey, three near Ciorli (sic) and five in the Smyrna area. Then, with no reference to German participation or presence, listeners were told: 'Rumanian fighters went into action when the alert sounded and attacked the bombers which were spread out, thus making a concentrated attack on them [the refineries] impossible. The Americans tried to hit their targets from a low level but were prevented by the fire of the anti-aircraft defences which brought down a number of the attackers in flames.' The broadcast concluded by explaining that the King and Queen Mother had visited those injured in the attack, as had Marshal Antonescu and members of the government, adding: 'The local population expressed their warm feeling for the Marshal'. Perhaps the need to report this alleged demonstration of affection was in itself an indication of the unpopularity of supporters of the Germans.

The Rumanian claim that anti-aircraft gunners were responsible for most of the B-24 losses over Ploesti was supported by Allied findings. Colonel Kane considered that the rear elements flew too high and therefore exposed themselves unnecessarily. An official American report, admitting that 'anti-aircraft gunfire was the principal cause of losses', thought the bomb-bay fuel tanks were 'the Liberator's Achilles heel . . . [and] a contributing [sic] factor of great importance'. If these had been emptied and dropped before the target 'no doubt . . . losses would have been smaller'. A few B-24s were certainly destroyed because of their vulnerable bomb-bay tanks – Second Lieutenant Hughes' aircraft at Campina is one example – but this was only one of several factors leading to the heavy losses. In reality it was a relatively minor one.

Major-General Brereton and more junior officers like Colonel Kane realised before the attack that heavy

ucharest. As Rumanians, fighting heir erstwhile allies, held a ring)und the capital, crews flew B-17s to Popesti airfield, barely stopping n the runway to haul their countrymen aboard.

Meanwhile in the immediate post-aid period enemy propaganda agen-es had been active. On 3rd August adio Bucharest broadcast details of a attack by 125 American bombers f the Flying Fortress type' against le oil region of Rumania two days arlier. It claimed that heavy anti-rcraft fire had prevented all but a w reaching their target. On the 'ound 147 had been wounded and 116 illed, sixty and sixty-three respec-vely in the women's prison demol-hed by one bomber. This report

**Evidence of attack on Romana
Americana, target White I**

losses might be incurred, but had held
that they would be worthwhile if
sufficient damage was achieved. It was
some time before a reasonable assessment of the results could be made, for
evidence came in slowly from many
different sources. Immediately, crew
reports given at debriefing were available, plus photographs taken during
the raid by cameras in the B-24s.
Overnight these reels were developed
and, on an appreciation of their evidence, Air Chief Marshal Tedder
signalled Brereton: 'A big job mag-
nificently done'. Shots of Columbia
Aquila (WHITE 5) showed B-24s
coming very low in formation and
passing between high towers. Many
fires could be seen, in particular in
camouflaged oil storage tanks, the
distillation plant appeared heavily
damaged and, in one photograph,
bombs could be seen falling in a horizontal position below an aircraft
flying at one hundred feet. Direct hits
at Steaua Romana (RED) were visible
on power plants and boiler houses,
with clouds of steam escaping from
the latter, and similar results were
perceived from photographs of Credituel Minier (BLUE) and Astra Romana
(WHITE 4). Apart from damage, these
photographs proved that the aircraft
did fly low: in particular, those of
WHITE 5 gave a clear picture of the
stepped up formations approaching
from the north-west as planned. In the
emotional aftermath of the attack
and with evidence like this, Tedder's
enthusiasm seemed appropriate and
a British preliminary assessment
dated 3rd August justified : 'Photographs taken during the raid show
BLUE, RED and WHITE 4 and 5
refineries well and truly hit and
WHITE 2 most probably.'

The same day an RAF Mosquito
carried out a photographic reconnaissance of the Ploesti area, but
owing to lack of fuel did not cover
Campina and Brazi. On 4th August

Lieutenant-Colonel Forster produced a report based on this evidence. Noting that 150-200 bombs (500-lb and 1,000-lb) had been dropped on Astra Romana and Unirea Orion (WHITE 4) he considered it doubtful if more than a dozen exploded 'as there are few signs of bomb-damaged plant, and fewer craters caused by mishits in or anywhere near the place'. This was also true of Concordia Vega (WHITE 2). He conceded, however, that the delayed-action fuses might have given the enemy bomb disposal teams time to dismantle many bombs. On 4th August, too, eye-witness accounts of the effects of the raid, transmitted through diplomatic and intelligence channels, began to arrive and cast doubt upon the accuracy of appreciations so far. From Istambul came a diplomatic message: 'According to casual eye-witnesses all important refinery plants in Ploesti and Campina destroyed or damaged except Romana Americana.' Three days later Istambul claimed that Targets BLUE (Brazi) and RED (Campina) had been 'destroyed', WHITE 4 (Astra Romana) and WHITE 5 (Columbia Aquila) 'severely damaged'. A preliminary estimate of the total damage was twenty milliard lei. The wisdom of careful evaluation of individual reports was underlined next day, however, when the same source claimed that WHITE 4, known to have been heavily damaged, and WHITE 2 (Concordia Vega), certainly hit by Major Appold's aircraft, were 'untouched'. This report thought that 'probably' only WHITE 5 (Columbia Aquila), RED and BLUE were badly hit and asserted that railway communications through Ploesti junction had been re-established after a mere six-hour delay. Other such information, notably that from a 'Hungarian Jewish dealer in oils and chemicals' who was in a train halted at Campina during the raid and later passed

through Ploesti, seems worthy of equally cautious treatment.

Some accounts were evidently more reliable than others. On 7th August Sir H Knatchbull-Hugessen transmitted information from Istambul to the Foreign Office in London which originated with the Turkish Ambassador in Bucharest. This stated that fires at Campina, Brazi and Ploesti were still burning on 3rd August, partly because the German fire-fighting services were 'ineffective'. There was some indication that 'mass emigration' from one devastated quarter of Campina had occurred, which revealed that all bombs had not fallen within the confines of the Steaua Romana refinery. But there was no indication as to whether the 'emigration' resulted from orderly evacuation or uncontrolled panic. The Turkish Ambassador reported that delayed-action bombs had caused considerable disruption to the repair squads and at Brazi had increased the initial four fires to twenty-four.

Nine days after the mission HQ RAF ME published 'the following information on the Ploesti raid [which] has been received from a reliable source in Rumania'. The Astra Romana refinery (WHITE 4) was 'partly out of action', with the Dubbs cracking plant seriously damaged, seven stores blown up, the aviation petrol plant destroyed and an estimated loss of output of 40 per cent. Romana Americana (WHITE 1) was untouched, but Concordia Vega (WHITE 2) also had its Dubbs cracking plant damaged, six stores blown up and a 30 per cent reduction in output. Steaua Romana (RED) had suffered 'complete destruction', Credituel Minier (BLUE) had 'vital sections destroyed' and Columbia (WHITE 5) an 80 per cent reduction in output. WHITE 3 (Unirea Sperantza and Standard Petrol Block) had received no damage, but Unirea Orion (within the confines of WHITE 4) had its 'stores completely destroyed' and half its

145

mineral oil production plant 'destroyed'.

Making use of all the information
so far available to it, on the same day
(10th August) HQ RAF ME concluded
that overall 70 per cent production
had been lost, much of it resulting
from the activation of delayed-action
bombs. This assessment continued:
'No serious damage to Ploesti town
. . . Accuracy of aim has astounded
Rumanians who state each bomb was
delivered at correct destination like
postal service'. It concluded: 'Reported crude oil will in future be
delivered to refineries in Germany
and Czechoslovakia'. Also on 10th
August, in a letter to Mr Berthoud of
the British Ministry of Fuel and
Power in London, Lieutenant-Colonel
Forster claimed that the Mosquito
reconnaissance photographs revealed
that up to 70 per cent of the delayed-
action bombs did not explode 'possibly
due to efficient bomb disposal, but
more probably due to rotten bombs'.
For this he blamed the USAAF. He
wrote that RAF officers had warned
the American authorities that standard fuses, which projected from the
rear of the bombs, would most probably suffer damage in a low-level
attack, because the bombs would fall
horizontally – a fact borne out by
raid photographs at Ploesti. The production of two assessments with some
contrary conclusions by British
sources on the same day underlined
the difficulty of reaching a balanced
evaluation on the effects of TIDAL-
WAVE.

On 13th August Lieutenant-Colonel
Forster produced an official report,
based upon the photographic evidence
from the raid of 1st August and the
reconnaissance of 3rd August, plus
information from 'an apparently

well-informed source'. Forster concluded that the aircraft bombed accurately and, although several bombs did not explode, a 'high degree' of short-term and 'a promising degree' of long-term damage had been achieved. The raid had therefore been on the whole 'very successful,' despite the absence of firm evidence about Campina and Brazi as yet. Even if the enemy had exaggerated the effect upon his production to mislead intelligence sources, Forster suggested that a 60 – 70 per cent shutdown 'for up to four weeks is a distinct possibility'. He pointed out that several refineries existed elsewhere in Rumania – for instance, five small refineries in the Ploesti area, one at Bucharest and one at Brasov – which had not been attacked. But the combined output capacity of all these amounted to only 3,500 tons per day and the difficulties of transportation (except from Ploesti and Bucharest) to distribution points were immense. At best all the small refineries could satisfy only 50–60 per cent of Rumania's internal requirements and he considered that the TIDALWAVE mission had caused 40–45 per cent long-term damage to the major refineries. When forwarding this report from Cairo HQ RAF ME reminded recipients that Forster 'is an expert on the technicalities of oil production [and] came to the Middle East to advise in the selection of specific targets in the various refineries, and to assess the results achieved'.

On 19th August another reconnaissance, this time by two Mosquitoes flying at 27–28,000 feet, obtained 'high level stereophotos' over Ploesti, Brazi and Campina. As a result, three days later Mr L Eisinger, Assistant Director of Industrial Production in the Ministry of State Middle East Supply Centre, produced a second more comprehensive assessment from Cairo. Forster's appreciation of damage to the WHITE targets was confirmed, but an estimate of the damage at RED and BLUE targets was now also possible.

Steaua Romana, Campina (RED) had its Stratford crude oil distillation group 'heavily damaged' and put out of action for probably six months, its boiler house and power plant were 'very heavily damaged' and expected to be out of action for a similar period. The asphalt plant was 'badly damaged' with repairs probably requiring four months, the paraffin-wax plant 'badly damaged' with six months needed for repairs 'if such could be undertaken at all' and 'the lubricating oil treating plant' was so 'badly damaged that it appears that repairs would hardly come into consideration'. 'Some damage' had occurred to the gasoline absorption plant and the fractionating equipment of the McKee Luboil Distilling Plant, whose wooden cooling tower had been 'destroyed', and 'some partial damage' had been caused to the Bruenn-Koenigsfelder Vacuum Luboil Distilling Plant: all these units, however, would probably be workable in two to three months. 'Heavy damage' had been caused to the oxygen plant, main workshop and storehouses, but, because of haze when the photographs were taken, the precise damage to the Dubbs plant was uncertain. 'Relatively little damage' was done to the tanks, one large and 'a few' small ones being burnt out.

At Credituel Minier (BLUE) the main fractionating column of the crude oil pipestill had 'collapsed' and, probably as a result, the reception installation and other auxiliary fractionating equipment had been damaged. It was 'unlikely' that this section of the refinery would be operational in less than four to six months. In addition the tank farm had suffered 'heavy damage', with four large and seventeen small tanks destroyed. There was evidence of some damage to the boiler house, main water cooling tower and offices, with 'light damage' to the Dubbs light oil furnace.

Eisinger considered the broad conclusion of Forster's first assessment 'quite correct'. Of the original refinery capacity of 24,750 tons per day in the seven targets, 10,360 (42 per cent) had been destroyed. To support this contention Eisinger estimated a total destruction at RED (3,400 tons), WHITE 5 (1,480) and BLUE (1,480) and a partial destruction at WHITE 2 (600/4,030) and WHITE 4 (3,400/6,760). In particular he emphasised the immobilisation of the cracking plants at BLUE, RED and WHITE 5, which he felt meant that 40 per cent of Rumania's total cracking capacity had been lost, and that Rumania's only paraffin-wax plant at RED had been 'put out of commission for a long period'. Eisinger sounded a note of caution, however, concerning lubricating oil. Accepting that the plant at RED had been virtually annihilated and the one at WHITE 4 was 'apparently heavily damaged', he considered that 'some repercussions on the supply position of lubricating oils would appear not to be excluded'. Nevertheless, the production of lubricating oil primarily depended upon the availability of 'asphaltic residue' and the deficiency in production would probably only be temporary.

Taking into consideration all the evidence, Eisinger therefore drew certain conclusions on the damage caused and its significance. Over 40 per cent of crude oil refining capacity and possibly 40 per cent (at least 30 per cent) of Rumania's cracking capacity had been knocked out for 'at least four probably six months'. However 'no direct consequence' was to be expected from this loss of crude oil refining capacity, as the balance left appeared 'more than sufficient to cope with Rumania's present crude oil output'. The loss of the paraffin-wax plant and the reduction of the production capacity of lubricating oil 'may cause some dislocation of present arrangements'. At RED and WHITE 5 there was no sign of activity. In his report Forster had suggested that the Germans may have sacrificed WHITE 5 by concentrating bomb disposal squads on WHITE 4 and rapid repair work now seemed underway at WHITE 4 (Astra Romana). Here use was apparently being made of old dated equipment, idle before the attack, and the 'normal number of tank wagons in the yard' suggested that loading operations were 'proceeding as usual'.

At Unirea Orion (part of WHITE 4) activity also seemed normal and therefore damage to the boiler house could not have been serious. But BLUE was at a standstill, though as the whole refinery relied upon the damaged pipestill, attempts at repair could be expected. At WHITE 2 the reconnaissance photographs showed no activity. Eisinger believed that there was no obvious reason for shutting this refinery down and suggested that the steam escapes may have been closed to mislead the Mosquitoes, whose presence had been detected. If Eisinger was right in this latter conclusion then part of the photographic evidence of 19th August and the validity of his own report must be open to question.

A meeting of the Target Information Branch, Operational Division, AC/AS, Intelligence, in Washington on 6th September was indeed cautious. In estimating the long-term damage to Rumanian refinery capacity as 42.5 per cent and drop in the annual refinery production from 9,235,000 to 5,300,000 tons, the meeting agreed that future refinery capacity 'will just suffice, or be slightly inadequate, to handle crude oil production . . . From the overall standpoint, therefore, the attack of 1st August 1943 destroyed the bulk of the cushion formed by the excess of *efficiently located* refinery capacity over crude oil production'. It concluded that 'rehabilitation', which it thus thought possible, would take six months.

During September and October information continued to arrive through various intelligence channels both on the effects of the raid itself and the restoration of production capacity.

On 18th September HQ RAF ME issued a digest of information 'from usually reliable sources'. This confirmed that Astra Romana (WHITE 4) had sustained damage to its power station and three out of four furnaces at the main distillation plant, and that 2,500 tons of oil had been lost through ruptured tanks. But an old distillation plant had been untouched and by mid-September it was expected to deal with about 3,000 tons per day; and electricity could be supplied from outside the refinery, pending repairs to the power station. Temporarily Romana Americana (WHITE 1), unaffected by the raid, was taking 1,500 tons of crude oil per day from Astra Romana, though to avoid congestion between wells and refineries 10,000 tons per day (in 1,000 tank cars) were being sent to Hungarian refineries. At Concordia Vega (WHITE 2) no serious damage had occurred, although late on the evening of 1st August a bomb had exploded, which fired six or seven crude oil tanks and destroyed about 6,000 tons of crude oil. An extensive overhaul of the refinery, which was necessary, would probably only halt production for two to three weeks.

The virtual destruction of Steaua Romana (RED) was confirmed. 2,000 tons of lubricating oil had been immediately lost and the destruction of the paraffin-wax plant deprived Germany of a considerable annual supply. It was impossible to say when production might be restored. The destruction of three or four storage tanks and serious damage to the pumping station had no effect in itself, as the refinery was out of action. No damage had been sustained by Standard Petrol Block and Unirea Sperantza (WHITE 3). However, installations in the former had been 'inactive . . . for some time' and would take 'some months' to get into working order. But the destruction at Credituel Minier (BLUE) was 'very serious'. Fifty-two bombs had hit the refinery and were directed on vital installations 'placed as if by hand'. It was estimated that 16,000 tons of crude oil had been destroyed and, most interestingly, that twenty of the sixty storage tanks had been hit by .50 machine-gun fire from the B-24s. Most of the refinery equipment was American and therefore impossible to replace during the war.

Information about Columbia Aquila (WHITE 5) revealed that at the time of the attack the refinery had been closed down for its annual overhaul, which explained the absence of burning tanks on the various photographs. But a large number of bombs had fallen on the distillation columns and cracking plant which had been practically razed to the ground. Lack of replacement equipment here, as at Brazi, might well put Columbia Aquila out of action for the rest of the war. During the raid the pipeline bringing crude oil to Ploesti from the oilfields burst near WHITE 2, but this was soon dealt with and no fire had developed.

According to this report the Rumanian government believed that the remaining refineries at Ploesti could cope immediately with 9,000 tons of crude oil per day, compared with an actual 15,000 (and theoretical 30,000) output before the raid. After 1st September it was hoped that 13,000 tons daily would be processed. However 13 per cent loss of distillation and 50 per cent of cracking capacity was admitted, with the result that only petrol was to be exported for the moment with all other refined products reserved for home use. Until the refineries were restored to full capacity a certain amount of crude oil would be sent to Hungary and Germany for refining. This RAF appreciation concluded that further attacks against the undamaged Romana Americana (WHITE 1) and Unirea Sperantza (WHITE 3) plus Astra Romana (WHITE 4) in the near future would prove 'disastrous' to the enemy.

Another cautious assessment of the situation occurred on 22nd September after Major O A Bell RASC, before the war assistant refinery manager at

Unirea Orion and Unirea Sperantza, had studied official reports and the raid photographs. He warned that estimates of damage must be made in accordance with the maximum possible output, not the pre-raid total. Hence Mr Eisinger should have listed the Unirea Orion capacity as 3,000 tons, not 1,280, per day. He believed that once the idle plant was activated in Ploesti only two to three weeks dislocation of production would occur. Specifically he pointed to the existence of eighteen boilers in the main Unirea Orion boiler house and the ease with which field boilers could temporarily replace those damaged. On 15th December 1939 a severe fire lasting ten hours had caused 'considerable damage' at this refinery, but it had been shut down for only ten days. Eisinger's estimate that a daily loss of 1,280 tons would occur at Unirea Orion for six months was far too optimistic.

Less than two months after TIDAL-WAVE it began to look, therefore, as if early claims of success had been considerably exaggerated. HQ RAF ME, quoting another 'reliable source', on 19th October stated: 'Refineries other than Steaua Romana (RED), Credituel Minier (BLUE) and Columbia Aquila (WHITE 5) have been repaired and refining capacity is now ,850 waggons per day. The above-mentioned concerns however were closed and will remain so until the end of the war'. Superficially this statement seems encouraging. But as each waggon carried 1,000 tons, in less than three months after TIDALWAVE the enemy output was already about 5 per cent of the pre-raid total. In addition, some crude oil was being treated in Hungary and Germany, though the loss of specialised products at RED and BLUE had proved a handicap to the enemy.

The Luftwaffe, in fact, claimed that though Ploesti was badly hit, its production soon returned to normal', and a USAAF appreciation of Spring 944 indirectly supported this view.

Pointing to the reactivation of idle plants, it concluded that TIDAL-WAVE had caused 'very heavy damage . . . [but] not sufficient to be decisive'. The problem was that Ploesti had always had about 40 per cent idle refinery capacity, which effectively meant that 41 per cent damage had to be caused before any impression could be made. And to assist in the reactivation process the Germans were able to bring in 10,000 slave labourers from occupied countries.

Summaries of Rumanian post-raid production make depressing reading. 410,000 tons of crude oil were processed by Rumanian refineries in July 1943. In August, the month of the raid, this figure dropped to 260,000, but in September had risen to 430,000 and in October even higher to 440,000. Total petrol exports were only slightly less impressive: exports to Germany are shown in brackets. In July 122,000 tons (100,000), August 70,000 (60,000), September 105,000 (100,000) and October 115,000 (105,000); and the figure in December exceeded that of July. The output of individual refineries was also unencouraging' from the Allied viewpoint. Astra Romana processed 120,000 tons in July, 54,000 in August, 144,000 in September and 165,000 in October. The undamaged Romana Americana processed 60,000 in July and 108,000 in August, then 75,000 and 70,000 in the ensuing two months respectively. Concordia Vega processed 60,000 in July, only 20,000 in August, but during September and October 75,000 and 80,000 respectively. Although unsatisfactory for the Allies, the recovery of output capacity in these refineries was to be expected at some stage. The speed of recovery did cause surprise, in particular at Steaua Romana (RED). Most intelligence assessments thought that this would be out of action for a lengthy period, if not the entire war. In July 45,000 tons were processed here and only 10,000 in August. Nothing was then produced for three months, but in December 10,000 and in January 1944 20,000 tons were dealt with. Although production thereafter did not exceed 30,000 tons in any one month, this represented approximately 70 per cent of the pre-raid total.

By early 1944 it was clear that original optimism about the effects of TIDALWAVE was indeed unwarranted. Yet there had been many warnings about the existence of idle refinery capacity at Ploesti, even as early as 1941 when a British Minister was still in Bucharest. None of the planners nor responsible RAF and USAAF advisers had claimed that one attack would neutralise the Ploesti refineries. At various times Major-General Brereton, Colonel Smart, Air Chief Marshal Sir Sholto Douglas and Air Chief Marshal Sir Arthur Tedder had specifically emphasised the need for follow-up missions to achieve a satisfactory result. Brigadier-General Ent had only forecast 50 per cent destruction with the loss of seventy-five aircraft and an intelligence appreciation thought that the same damage would be caused for the loss of seventy-one out of 200 aircraft. As it emerged, despite tactical troubles on the day, less aircraft were actually lost and the overall damage achieved was not far short of that anticipated. Moreover, much more heavy damage was done to BLUE, RED and WHITE 5 than pre-raid forecasts predicted. If WHITE 1 and WHITE 3 had been attacked at all and WHITE 2 as planned, the raid could have had more success than its own planners envisaged.

Events on the day were therefore of vital importance. Later authorities have blamed many aircraft losses at Ploesti on faulty navigation. Lieutenant-Colonel Forster, nine days after the raid, heavily criticised execution of the attack. He complained that: 'It seems quite impossible to teach the Americans anything – they always know better than other people with wide experience': the successful aspects of the mission resulted from close attention to what he and RAF Officers had said. Bitterly he ex-claimed: 'It was a great pity, for all the fine men who lost their lives needlessly. I am absolutely convinced that if the RAF had done the task, they would have put all the seven refineries completely out of action for at least six months and probably much longer'. In passing on this letter to the Air Ministry 'with a certain diffidence,' the Ministry of Fuel and Power drew attention to 'its rather free style'. Its implications and assertions were, in fact, grossly unfair. There is no guarantee that the RAF, even if the means had been at its disposal, could have done a more effective job. Perhaps such letters, with their overtones of chauvinistic arrogance are best left unwritten.

Nevertheless, however unjust such scathing comments might be, the performance of mission crews needs examination. The courage of all those who flew to Ploesti, including Target Force WHITE 1 which did contend with considerable defensive fire before breaking off its attack, should not be doubted. Even a superficial glance at the raid photographs must immediately silence sceptics, unwilling to believe that such a low-level attack was actually carried out. Five Congressional Medals of Honour (Colonels Johnson and Kane, Lieutenant-Colonel Baker, Major Jerstad and Second Lieutenant Hughes), fifty-six Distinguished Service Crosses (including Brigadier-General Ent, Colonels Compton and Wood, Lieutenant-Colonel Posey and Major Appold), forty-one Silver Stars, one Bronze Oak Leaf Cluster to the Silver Star, 136 Bronze Oak Leaf Clusters to the Distinguished Flying Cross, 1,320 Distinguished Flying Crosses and one Soldier's Medal were awarded to TIDALWAVE participants. In addition Colonel Smart gained the Distinguished Service Medal, Lieutenant-Colonel Forster, Major Geerlings, Group Captain Lewis and

The result of a follow-up mission by RAF Halifaxes and Wellingtons

Wing Commander Streater the Legion of Merit, and all the bombardment groups involved received citations. Undoubtedly both planners and aircrew deserved these awards for their dedication and effort.

That the Fifteenth Air Force had to carry out twenty daylight raids and 205 Group (RAF) four night raids on Ploesti between 5th April and 19th August 1944 is no real indication of failure on 1st August 1943. For instant success with one raid had not been expected. However, TIDALWAVE losses suggested that a sustained bombing campaign could not be carried out on Rumanian targets until closer bases had been established. On 17th August Colonel Smart declared that 'subsequent attacks on the Ploesti refineries are necessary', but pointed out that precise information about the damage already caused must be gained by British and American agents in Rumania. Furthermore to exploit that damage operations must be carried out to interfere with the passage of crude oil and refined products to Germany and Czechoslovakia, possibly by mining the Danube, reaching the dam at Passau (by a similar mission to that on the Moehne and Eder dams) or destroying the locomotives which pulled barges through the Iron Gates on the Lower Danube. The Combined Chiefs of Staff, however, were not enthusiastic given available resources and the results of 1st August. On their recommendation President Roosevelt and Winston Churchill agreed 'later' to approach Stalin about the possibility of Russian action instead.

In a broader context the whole aim of USAAF strategic bombing was once more called into question. Air Chief Marshal Harris, always an opponent of selective precision bombing, claimed that Ploesti proved this to be impracticable. It was impossible to bring an enemy to his knees by concentrating on one or more of his industries, like oil or ball bearings. People who held this view were 'panacea mongers', not conversant with the harsh realities of war. But all TIDALWAVE proved was that the one low-level attack carried out in this fashion could not neutralise the Ploesti refineries.

Brereton later claimed that bad weather and errors of judgement on the day, particularly Ent's decision to attack from the south (which he considered 'unsound') ruined the plan. If 'executed as planned at least 90 per cent success would have been obtained and combat losses would have been minimised'. There is no doubt that several unforeseen incidents did grossly affect the TIDALWAVE mission. The division of the mission force into two sections over Albania and Jugoslavia was the first important occurrence, followed by delay after Colonel Kane's wrong appreciation of the situation on reaching the Danube. For none of this could Brigadier-General Ent be blamed, even if the leading two groups were left of the correct course over Jugoslavia as Kane claimed. Colonel Kane himself must take some blame for this. Twice he failed to follow 93 Group when cloud was encountered: once he led his and the trailing groups through the cloud, once under it. So the fatal gap opened up unbeknown to the mission commander.

Brigadier-General Ent's mis-identification of Targovesti was certainly important, but in fairness visibility was bad and Targoviste very like Floresti from the air. Its distinctiveness had prompted Colonel Williamson to recommend it to Colonel Smart as an Initial Point at an early stage of planning. Ent must have realised his error, but to his credit did not panic into a hasty counter-order, which could have caused confusion and fatal mid-air collisions. In a sense he made the best of his error by bringing both groups onto an orderly approach run towards Ploesti, though his swing to

its smother the Ploesti railway during an attack by Fifteenth Air Force, April 1944

the east must remain something of a mystery. There was no reason not to contact Lieutenant-Colonel Baker leading 93 Group if he was trying to pick up Floresti by skirting Ploesti. Radio silence had no meaning with 88mm shells whistling skywards and machine-gun bullets from fighters spraying the bombers. But his subsequent route with 376 Group suggests that he was trying to find WHITE 1 and possibly expecting Baker to follow him without question to locate his own WHITE 2 and 3. Perhaps this lack of communication between Bucharest and Ploesti was even more important than the original wrong turn. For Ent's 'MS' (Mission Successful) signal, however, there seems no rational explanation.

The discipline of the two groups, which followed Ent from Targoviste, and the 389th, which allowed Colonel Wood to correct his own navigational error short of Campina, suggests that a smaller force might have been more manageable and relatively more successful. The achievements of Colonels Kane and Johnson and Lieutenant-Colonel Posey underline this. In fact, TIDALWAVE was too ambitious, five groups too many to keep together over such a prolonged flight. Neither Ent's error nor unfavourable weather conditions were primarily responsible for the destruction of a plan which from the outset contained serious inherent dangers. Specifically, the imposition of radio silence is difficult to justify. Both Brereton and Smart stated that the low-level nature and the north-westerly direction of the attack would create surprise. But in addition radio silence, which might have made Ent aware of the problems over Jugoslavia and stopped Kane from lingering over the Danube, was decreed to avoid detection. This pre-

Devastation at the Astra Romana, December 1944

supposed a lack of observation and communication in enemy-occupied countries. The B-24s were spotted crossing the Albanian coast and later evidence revealed that the enemy was aware of their presence thereafter. To hope otherwise was to indulge in unrealistic pipe dreams. The planners, by aiming for both secrecy of approach and surprise in the attack, seemed to discount enemy capability outside the immediate target area.

In outline on the drawing board and over the Cyrenaican desert TIDALWAVE undoubtedly appeared feasible. But bombing missions are carried out in dangerous combat conditions and often in adverse weather conditions. The impression that a battlefield on land or in the air resembles a chessboard is reserved for romantic historians. It has never had much basis in fact. Early in the 19th Century the Prussian military theorist Karl von Clausewitz emphasised this by allowing for 'friction' in warfare.

TIDALWAVE planners allowed themselves to be seduced by the size of the prize apparently within their grasp. Economically the mission might seem attractive, militarily it was impracticable. Air Chief Marshal Tedder was right to express his 'deep admiration . . . [for] the gallantry and determination with which the attacks were pressed home', and General Arnold to signal Brereton: 'We are all immensely proud of the showing you made'. But Arnold continued less soundly: 'The impression prevails that TIDALWAVE dealt a blow that will contribute materially to the defeat of the Axis'. Unhappily it did not.

Meticulously planned and courageously carried out TIDALWAVE was a costly failure. In truth its supporters had not predicted success without follow-up missions and it was not their fault that these were delayed for over nine months. Air Chief Marshal Tedder exaggerated when he claimed that 'the operation compensated amply for the disappointment of the

first attack [Halpro] on the Ploest refineries'. General Eisenhower com mented more pithily: 'As usual mathe matical calculations could not wi over unexpected conditions'.

Reviewing TIDALWAVE, Majo General Brereton concluded: 'N blame is attached to any commande or leader participating in the missior for decisions which were made on th spot under the stress of combat Colonel Smart declared: 'It is easy fo football fans to sit back on Monda morning [and] play quarterback maintaining that 'human error wil happen in any manoeuvres'. Unfor tunately human fallibility unde stress was not suddenly revealed o 1st August 1943: it has been evident i warfare since time immemorial. Th ability to take decisions in comba situations, which involve the lives c others and the success of a mission, i the prime requirement of a senic officer. But the limits within whic

A B-24 heads home after a successful raid on Ploesti

le has to operate are also relevant and planners must be aware of human, natural and military factors when formulating their ideas.

Brigadier-General Ent feared the cost of a low-level mission, so did many others, including Brereton and Smart; and Brereton's decision to use this tactic only followed a careful consideration of alternatives. Yet nobody appeared to consider fully the dangers inherent in getting such a large force over enemy territory into position to attack such a distant target. Too much attention was concentrated on tactical details from the initial Points to the targets; too little thought was devoted to possible problems on the approach route. To blame individuals like Major-General Brereton or Colonel Smart for this would be invidious.

Defects in the TIDALWAVE plan may be ascribed to lack of experience by USAAF personnel in this type of operation at this stage of the war. They may be explained by the stubborn American belief in the self-defending bomber, which, despite ample evidence to the contrary, persisted until the second disastrous raid on Schweinfurt in Bavaria in October 1943. But the bravery of those who flew to Ploesti on 1st August 1943 should not be questioned. The air battle which took place in Rumanian skies on that summer Sunday was indeed epic. An unwitting, certainly unintended compliment to the airmen's courage was paid by a Bulgarian newspaper when, shortly after the mission, it declared that the United States government had offered 10,000 dollars, medals and extra leave as inducement for crews to fly that day.

Bibliography

Military Operations in Macedonia, Vol 1 C Falls (London 1933)
The Army Air Forces in World War II, Vol 2 W F Craven & J L Cate (ed) (Chicago, 1949)
Ploesti J Dugan & C Stewart (London, 1963)
The Mighty Eighth R A Freeman (London, 1970)
The Economic Blockade, Vols 1 & 2 W N Medlicott (London, 1952-9)
Oil: A Study of War-time policy and Administration D J Payton-Smith (London, 1971)
The Strategic Air Offensive against Germany 1935-1945, Vols 1, 2 & 4 C Webster & N Frankland (London, 1961)
Low Level Attack L Wolff (London, 1957)